PERSONAL SERVICES

First published in Great Britain in 1987 by
Pavilion Books Limited
196 Shaftesbury Avenue, London WC2H 8JL
in association with Michael Joseph Limited
27 Wrights Lane, Kensington, London W8 5TZ

Introduction © Terry Jones 1987
Original screenplay by David Leland
© Zenith Productions Limited 1986
Colour photographs © Mike Laye 1987
Other material © Zenith Productions Limited 1987

Designed by Lawrence Edwards
Stills photography by Mike Laye

British Library Cataloguing in Publication Data
Leland, David
    Personal services.
    I. Title
    791.43'72   PN1997

    ISBN 1-85145-146-3

Printed in Great Britain by
Butler & Tanner Ltd, Frome and London

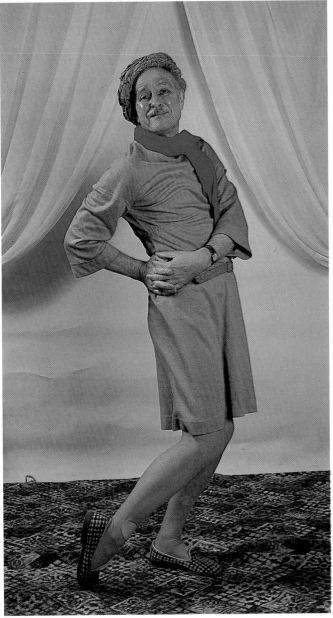

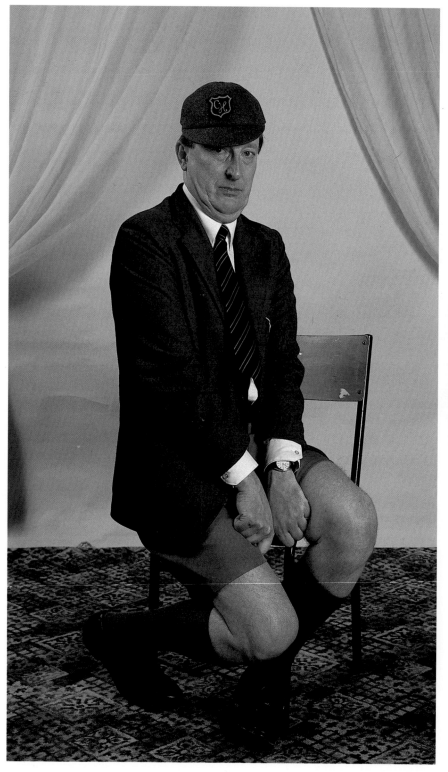

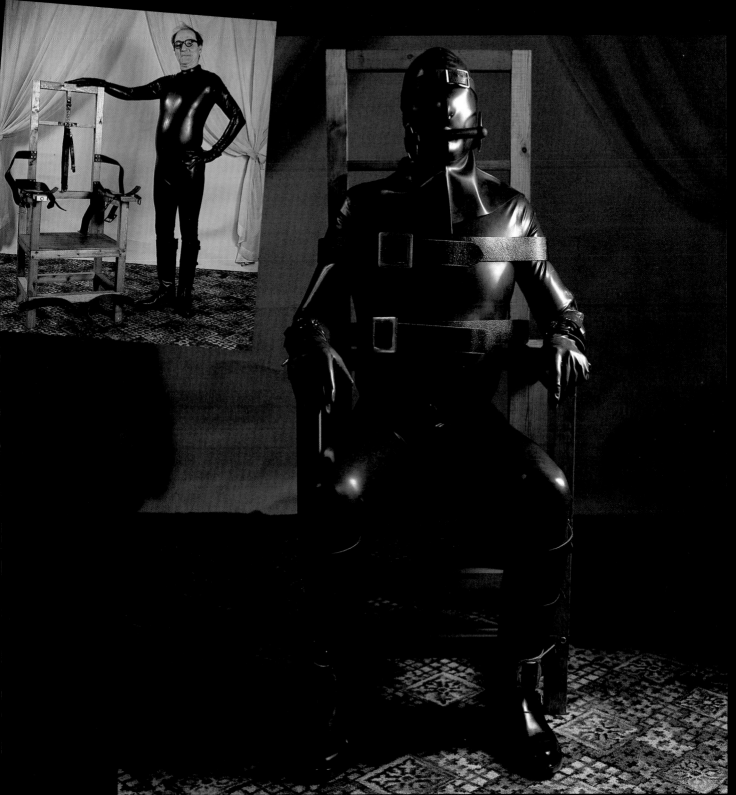

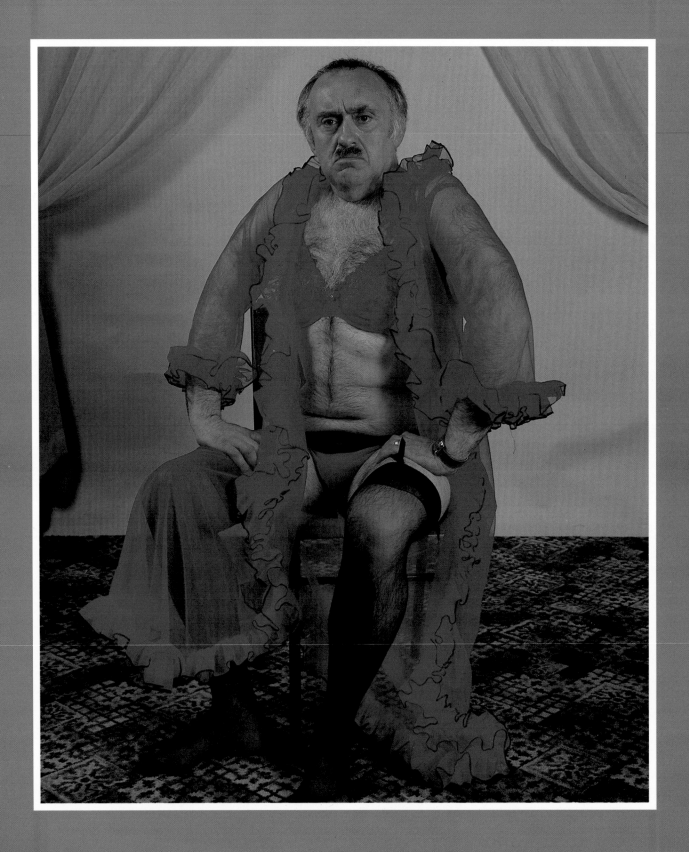

JULIE WALTERS – Christine   DANNY SCHILLER – Dolly

THE PRINCIPAL PLAYERS

'Julie Walters is a phenomenon,' says Alec McCowen. 'Along with Maggie Smith and Glenda Jackson, she has that extraordinary energy which is quite bewildering.' She worked harder than anybody, but never complained about a thing.'

'I like working,' says Julie. 'we'd work fifteen hours some days. You'd get home and think about washing your hair, and the next second you'd be asleep. And then up again at five. I didn't have a day off for eight weeks.' She enjoyed the dressing up immensely. 'It's funny the effect different costumes had on people; what turned some on and not others. Most of the men liked the schoolgirl, but it was who liked the PVC girl that was most interesting; always the people you wouldn't think would.'

'When I first read the script I loved it, but I found it a really difficult part to begin with. I couldn't understand what David Leland was saying about certain scenes. I could *intellectually*, but . . . Then I discovered how to play the part. It's like everything that's difficult, and that you eventually crack. The last bit was easier, because Christine was more of an assured woman and her own 'performance' was more polished. It's about a transition into something else: suddenly becoming a person who knows what she wants and is going to get it. It's one of the most enjoyable films I've done.'

'Danny had been dreading the willy scene,' says Julie Walters. 'We had a couple of glasses of wine before we did it. Then I thought David was joking when he said they had to re-shoot it, because they couldn't see Danny's willy.' But Schiller didn't baulk. He might have felt a bit awkward, but he had no reservations about the film. 'It was a unique part,' he says. 'Very nice. I'd never played anything like it. I normally play little comic victims, or spiky outsiders.'

The success of the willy scene depends on Danny having already convinced the viewers that he is an ordinary woman, and Dolly is the typical middle-aged, working class mum, modestly dressed, slow and comfortable. 'She looks like the woman next door,' says Schiller. He has a Polaroid of himself sitting outside London's County Hall, dressed in a blue coat and hat, floral dress, white shoes and handbag. 'I sat there for at least an hour and no one gave me a second glance. I wanted to see what people thought . . . and they didn't think anything.'

When the *Personal Services* script dropped through Peter Cellier's Surrey letterbox, he thought 'Good God, I can't do this!' But after listening to Mary Whitehouse, the anti-obscenity campaigner, for an hour on his car radio, he was so incensed that when he arrived for the audition he said 'I'm here, take me, I'll do it!'

'I don't think it's important whether a film about prostitution is made or not. What I do think is important is that someone should be allowed to make one if they want to. Mary Whitehouse is continually saying she's concerned for children, but its no use trying to protect children from what they are bound to meet sooner or later. The only answer is to educate them and instil in them a sense of responsibility, firstly to themselves and secondly to their fellow human beings. That's the way to create a better moral atmosphere.'

He enjoyed making the film. 'I've never had so much fun on a film before. They dressed me up as a big schoolboy. I just collapsed on the studio floor at one point in total hysterical laughter. We laughed for about ten minutes. Wonderful! But I don't play the part for laughs – it goes much deeper than that. I don't find the film offensive; I find it rather true to life.'

'When I first read the part of Shirley in the script,' says Shirley Stelfox, 'I thought "I know that lady!". I knew how she ticked. She was so warm, so marvellous, yet there she was, a "lady of the night". She's happily married, with a lovely, warm husband, and yet she deals with the kinks. Suddenly I understood her capacity to be able to separate herself from her job and yet at the same time have an element of compassion for the people she deals with. I thought "If they're giving me one iota of a chance for this character, there'll be no one to beat me".' She got the part.

'We had to wear ridiculous things like unbelievably high heels. All that dressing up and tarting up was very strange. Just the sight of Julie made me laugh so much . . . to see her tottering along in yet another outrageous costume. She had a black, shiny cat suit and these boots . . . black, shiny things and, bless her heart, she looked deformed because they hurt her so much! If anyone could have seen us, with me saying "Bend the knees slightly . . . drop the bum in"!

'This was a rare film, like a theatre company who has become very close and caring. When people came in to play small parts, everybody would try to make them relaxed and happy. I'm sure that's what the major movies that have millions spent on them lack. They lose that wonderful feeling of "the play's the thing".'

At sixty, Anthony Collin is probably the definitive small government official. Short, fat and balding, he has four principal acting modes – benevolent or evil, glasses on or glasses off – and most of his parts seem to have called for one permutation of these or another. Mr Webb is an unusual variation on the theme, and at first, he says, '. . . I was a little apprehensive. But as soon as I realised I could be naughty rather than lascivious I felt better . . .

'There was a wonderful atmosphere about the place. To see all those respected actors who, half an hour before, had been talking about agents and offers for *Dynasty* – and there they were in drag and dressed as schoolboys – was quite something!'

ARTHUR WHYBROW – Mac

ALEC McCOWEN – Ex-Wing Commander Morten

LEON LISSEK – Mr Popozogolou

The most disagreeable thing actress Shirley Stelfox was asked to do in the film was to seal up 63-year-old Whybrow in a tight rubber suit and lock him in a wooden box. 'This outfit covered him completely,' she says. 'Then we put a mask on him. There was a mouth-hole cut into it just big enough for him to breathe and then I had to put this heavy rubber thing – like a dog bone – in his mouth and tighten it with straps round his head. Then he was locked in a cupboard. It was awful.' Arthur takes up the story. 'I feel sorry for people like this. I wonder if there is a way to make it easier for them. Is there some help, some sort of medical treatment? Because a bloke who does what I had to do in the film definitely needs help.'

Arthur's not sure about *Personal Services:* 'I don't know whether it's right, but I don't see there's anything a great deal wrong with it. But I didn't see anything funny about sitting in the cupboard, I didn't see anything funny in that at all. This is a serious film.'

Alec McCowen is a respected writer and actor who, at 61, is not generally known for his unconventional roles. A gentle man, he inhabits a conservative burgundy pullover in a respectable Kensington flat, and indulges in only the most innocuous of vices – such as spending a whole day reading magazines. So it was with a sense of mischief that he was able to tell his neighbour, who was leaving for the office one morning, that he had spent the night in a police van with nineteen prostitutes! 'A bit of healthy vulgarity is very refreshing,' he says. 'It was a relief to do *Personal Services.*

'The Wing Commander came out of the closet and I feel that, by playing him, I've come out of the closet as an actor, too. Occasionally as an actor you discover yourself when you find you're doing something far outside your expectations and the normal run of things. I found that happening to me when I was being led into that cell yelling and struggling between two policemen.'

'After forty years of acting I'm fairly unsentimental, but I found at the end of the film, when the time came for me to say goodbye, that I was very moved and near to tears. It had been enormous fun – I felt as though I'd been to a terrific party, and it will go down as one of the finest memories in my working life!'

Lissek is forty-seven and something of a hybrid: an Australian-bred child of mixed Greek and Polish parentage, he speaks with an English Oxford accent.

In *Personal Services* he plays Christine's landlord, Mr Popozogolou, who receives payment of rent 'in kind'. 'If I'd thought the film was pornographic, I'd have pulled back, but it isn't. It's entertaining and has an insight. Even so, I don't think I've ever been in anything quite so risqué.

'One of the big bonuses about this film was Julie Walters, who is an absolute delight. Within minutes of her arriving people would be laughing and cracking jokes. Then, as soon as you started to rehearse, that was it – complete concentration.'

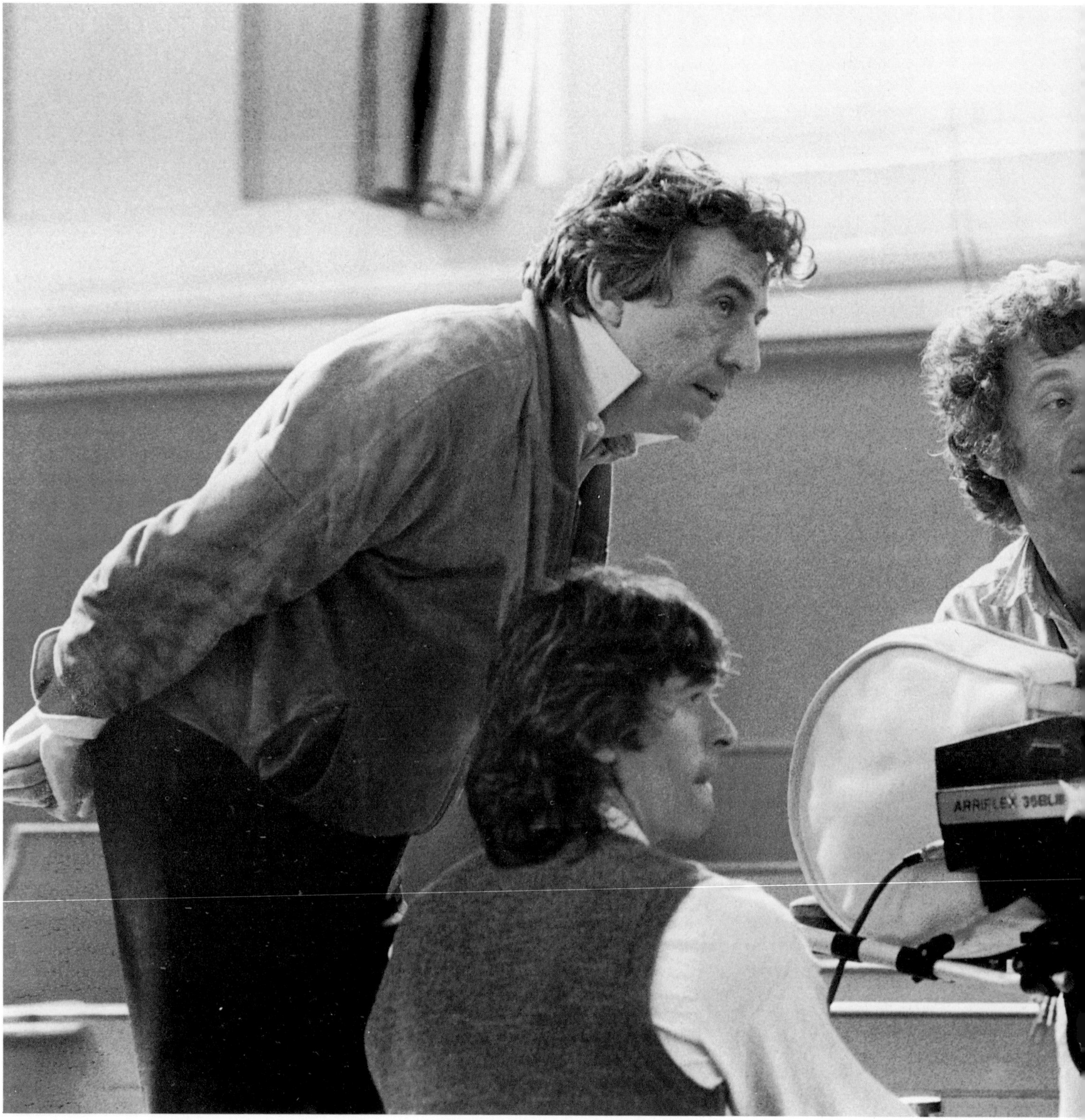
ARRIFLEX 35BL

INTRODUCTION

I first read the script of *Personal Services* when I was on holiday in the summer of '85. Or, rather, I tried to read it, but every time I put it down for five seconds somebody else snapped it up, and wouldn't let go of it until they'd read it from cover to cover. So I knew, before I'd read a single word of it, that *Personal Services* held a more than common amount of human interest. Indeed, it was *so* full of human interest that my eleven-year-old daughter had read it three times before I'd even realised it was all about the catering industry!

When I did finally manage to read the script, however, I agreed with my daughter that it was funny, true and portrayed the human sexual condition in a raw, unvarnished manner that neither of us had come across before. I remember thinking: 'I wouldn't mind directing that,' but I didn't think it very seriously, because another director had already started casting and was all set to begin filming it.

However, 1985 being British Film Year, it was becoming increasingly difficult to get a British film off the ground. Stars and film-makers alike were far too busy touring embryonic bingo halls in the provinces and attending champagne buffets to be distracted by modest projects about suburban brothels . . . and, besides, the Government had finally demonstrated its determination to establish a healthy British film industry by removing all incentives to investment in it. So *Personal Services* remained on the tarmac. Director, actors and animal trainers alike found other flights of fancy, and David Leland (with whom I was working on something else at the time) suddenly asked me if I'd like to do it.

By then, of course, most of the reputable film-makers in the country had turned it down in favour of setting-up a long-term series of British Film Year Champagne Dinner-Dance 'Bring and Buy' Sales in Basingstoke, but I couldn't refuse. My daughter said she'd never speak to me again if I didn't do it, and my lawyer said he'd never speak to me again if I did. So I was well and truly hooked.

We started casting in November 1985, and are still trying to finalise the list. However, in the meantime, the film appears to have been made, and by the time you hold this book in your hands it has probably been shown six times on Algerian TV, and is now being used as spacing by the editor of *Aliens 24*.

Nonetheless, I hope you enjoy reading this script as much as my family and friends and travel agent did in that long ago summer of '85 in the heart of Gascony. I hope also that you get as brown reading it.

Terry Jones, September 1986

Director Terry Jones linked to producer Tim Bevan.

Writer David Leland with Christine,
played by Julie Walters.

PERSONAL SERVICES   By David Leland

THE FILM

British Screen and Zenith
present
A Zenith Production

PERSONAL SERVICES

JULIE WALTERS
ALEC McCOWEN
SHIRLEY STELFOX

Written by
DAVID LELAND

Produced by
TIM BEVAN

Directed by
TERRY JONES

Consultant – Cynthia Payne

This film is a fiction. The author's
inspiration was a book about Cynthia
Payne. However, the events recorded
in the film, and the characters who
appear in it are wholly fictitious. The
true story of Cynthia Payne can be
found in *An English Madam* by Paul
Bailey.

Note: The screenplay contains some
scenes which do not appear in the
final version of the film.

Lunchtime.

Near Victoria Station, the New Victoria is quite a large café catering for TRAVELLERS, COMMUTERS, TAXI DRIVERS, *and it is sometimes frequented by* PROSTITUTES *who work in the area. It is owned and run by* BENITO, *an Italian in his fifties.*

The lunchtime rush is on and the café is very busy.

CHRISTINE, *a waitress, is having an on-the-hoof conversation with* JACKIE *(20), another waitress. They are constantly on the move.*

CHRISTINE *is 32 years old. She comes from a lower aspiring to middle-class background. She is bright and friendly. Naïve, but not a fool. Her voice can cut through almost anything. She is conventional in her dress, somewhat old-fashioned in her style. She is wearing a black and white waitress's uniform.*

The kitchen door smashes open, CHRISTINE *and* JACKIE *burst into the café laden with plates of food, gravy spills from the plates carried by* CHRISTINE.

> CHRISTINE
> What is it? What does it mean?
>
> JACKIE
> What?
>
> CHRISTINE
> DIY
>
> JACKIE
> Do It Yourself.
>
> CHRISTINE
> I know!

JACKIE *laughs.* CHRISTINE *is very curious.*

She wipes off a gravy stained thumb print from the edge of a plate before giving it to the CUSTOMER.

> CHRISTINE
> But it's not plumbing, is it? It's not messing about with Black and Decker drills.

JACKIE
It might be.

CHRISTINE
Tell me!

Bang – through the door into the kitchen. Crashing activity, a sweatshop.

JACKIE
Do It Yourself.

CHRISTINE
I know!

JACKIE
That's what it is.

CHRISTINE
What?!

JACKIE
Do It Yourself!

They dump their dirty crocks and collect meals on plates.

CHRISTINE
I still don't get it.

JACKIE *whispers into* CHRISTINE*'s ear, moves on, leaves her standing.*

CHRISTINE
Oh! I see! Do it yourself!
(laughs, thinks it's hilarious)
That's filthy, really filthy! How do you know that? I didn't
know. How do you know these things?

JACKIE – *Bang! – through the door into the café, delivering meals to tables.*

CHRISTINE
(follows Jackie)
And O-levels. What's O-levels?

JACKIE
Shh!

CHRISTINE
Why? Why shush? O-levels are exams. That's what my
David's doing, at his private school, he's doing O-levels.

JACKIE *moves to another table.*

JACKIE
What was yours, sir?

JACKIE *takes the orders.* CHRISTINE *goes over to* JUNE *(46) who takes
the cash at the till.*

> **CHRISTINE**
> Do you enjoy it, June?

> **JUNE**
> What?

> **CHRISTINE**
> Sex.

> **JUNE**
> When I get it, what about you?

> **CHRISTINE**
> Wet knickers and missed periods. The first time I had it I thought I'd been knocked down by a brewer's dray.

CHRISTINE *sees somebody out of the café window.*

> **CHRISTINE**
> Oi! Eh!!

CHRISTINE *runs out of the café to try to stop* ROSE. ROSE, *a rather thin, scrawny woman wearing a short leather skirt and jacket, is pushing an old Silver Cross pram. She is about to come into the café, but sees* CHRISTINE *and makes a run for it.*

---

2   EXT.   THE NEW VICTORIA CAFE   DAY

ROSE *beetles off down the street with the pram,* CHRISTINE *shouts after her.*

> **CHRISTINE**
> Eh! Rose — you bugger! You owe me rent! Bloody tart.

CHRISTINE *runs back into the café just as a large Bentley pulls up at the front door.*

---

3   INT.   NEW VICTORIA CAFE   DAY

CHRISTINE *runs behind the counter to collect her coat.*

> **CHRISTINE**
> (to Jackie)
> Can you cover for me? I've got to go out.

> **JACKIE**
> What — now?

4   EXT.   THE NEW VICTORIA CAFE   DAY

SYDNEY *(late fifties), a small corpulent man with a very shiny bald head, gets out of the Bentley and walks into the New Victoria café. He is smoking a very large cigar.*

5   INT.   THE NEW VICTORIA CAFE   DAY

SYDNEY *gives a friendly wave to* JUNE *as he enters the café.* JACKIE *walks out from behind the counter carrying two cups of tea.*

> JUNE
> BCSD.

> JACKIE
> BCSD.

JACKIE *does a smart about turn.* CHRISTINE *has her coat on and is about to leave the café.*

> JACKIE
> Christine. BCSD.

> CHRISTINE
> Oh, Christmas.

CHRISTINE *bustles out of the kitchen carrying a plate of roast beef and two veg., knife, fork and spoon, glass of water and a serviette.*

She walks quickly over to SYDNEY, *wipes the plate where her thumb has slipped into the gravy, and puts the plate of food in front of him.*

> SYDNEY
> Thanks, babe. What about tonight?

> CHRISTINE
> What about the weekend?

> SYDNEY
> The Dorchester.

> CHRISTINE
> David's sports day.

> SYDNEY
> Dinner and dance.

Having cleaned the utensils on her apron, she plonks them down on either side of the plate of food.

> CHRISTINE
> (not very enthusiastic)
> Very nice.

SYDNEY
Put your best frock on.

Watched by SYDNEY, CHRISTINE *heads for the exits, passing* JACKIE *as she goes.*

JACKIE
BCSD?

CHRISTINE
BCSD.

6   EXT.   THE NEW VICTORIA CAFE   DAY

CHRISTINE *walks, half runs, out of the café, searching her handbag as she goes — can't find what she's looking for — stops, heads back in the opposite direction.*

7   INT.   CHRISTINE'S FLAT   DAY

CHRISTINE*'s flat is small: single bedroom, single bed, living-room, kit. and bath, furn. accommodation, to rent.*

P.O.V. from the front door down the hall *towards the* bathroom. *Pinned on the bathroom door is a large colour poster of Prince Charles and Lady Diana.*

DOLLY *is on the phone in the hall.* DOLLY *is of indeterminate age; plump, droll, moves quite slowly and does not set out to look attractive.*

DOLLY
(on the phone)
Ginette is twenty-two. She has a full but firm 36.24.36
figure and offers a full personal service. You will like her.

CUT TO:

8   INT.   STAIRS   DAY

TOP SHOT: CHRISTINE *races up the stairs passing* MR MARPLES, *a middle-aged man.*

CUT TO:

9   INT.   CHRISTINE'S FLAT   DAY

CAMERA moves past DOLLY *towards the bathroom, past Charles and Diana, into the bedroom. In the bedroom is* SHIRLEY, *dressing in front of a full-length wardrobe mirror. Somewhat incongruously, there is a tin helmet and gas-mask on the chair; also a dunce's cap, a mortar-board and a large rubber apron.*

SHIRLEY *is in her mid-thirties; nothing fazes her. She has a dry sense of humour – a warm, generous and attractive woman.*

> DOLLY
> (still on the phone)
> Ginette has breathtaking revealing photos, caters for party lovers and offers a full theatrical wardrobe, French maid, nurse, gymslip, that kind of thing, mild CP and other games. Executive fun for the over forties.

A ring on the doorbell.

> DOLLY
> Kinky but not cruel. Why not pop round? Good. Bye, bye.

DOLLY *hangs up the phone as she opens the front door.* CHRISTINE *dashes into the flat.*

> CHRISTINE
> Forgot my keys.

CHRISTINE *grabs a large bunch of keys from near the telephone – where a photograph of herself with her son,* DAVID, *can be seen.*

> CHRISTINE
> See you later. Make yourself at home. Ha, ha.

CHRISTINE *dashes back out of the front door, almost bumping into* MR MARPLES *as she goes.*

> CHRISTINE
> Oops! Excuse me.

> MR MARPLES
> (to Dolly)
> Good afternoon.

> DOLLY
> Good afternoon.

MR MARPLES *walks into the flat. He is tall, smart, he is wearing a well tailored three-piece suit. He is carrying a large briefcase. His whole demeanour echoes somewhere quite different and more luxurious. He does not belong here.*

> DOLLY
> You have an appointment with the Governess, is that correct?

> MR MARPLES
> No, that is not correct. I have an appointment with the Nanny.

MR MARPLES *opens the door which leads into the bathroom. He locks the door from within.*

SHIRLEY *comes out of the bedroom dressed as* 'THE MISTRESS OF THE HOUSE OF PAIN'.

> DOLLY
> (to Shirley)
> Mr Marples for the Nanny.
>
> SHIRLEY
> I thought Mr Marples was House of Pain.
>
> DOLLY
> (shakes head)
> Winkie poos and bot-bots.
>
> SHIRLEY
> Oh, God, it's taken me an hour to get into this lot.

SHIRLEY *pulls off her wig, revealing her own hair beneath.*

10 EXT. STREET DAY
___

CHRISTINE *walks past the café, past the Bentley –* SYDNEY *looks up as she passes by, he's still tucking into his meat and two veg.*

Coat over her waitress's uniform, still beating the clock, CHRISTINE *walks along the street through a busy street market. She fails to notice* ROSE'S BABY *sitting in its Silver Cross pram parked outside a shop.*

CHRISTINE *arrives at the front door of a delapidated building, rubbish from the market piled high. She shoves open the front door and heads up the stairs, kicking rubbish out of the way as she goes. She looks through the letter-box, produces the large bunch of keys from her handbag, unlocks the door, kicks it at the bottom, and it opens.*

11 INT. ROSE'S FLAT DAY
___

CHRISTINE *lets herself into a one-bedroom flat. It's empty and in a mess. Post (circulars) on the mat. She is looking for* ROSE, *but the flat is empty.*

12 EXT. STREET DAY
___

ROSE, *pushing her* BABY *in the Silver Cross pram, arrives at the flat. Fruit and veg. and a large box of soap powder piled up on the pram. She parks the pram outside the front door near the cardboard boxes, and heads up the exterior staircase.*

Bert Kaempfert MUSIC.

CLOSE-UP of a penthouse suite in the clouds, a real-life dream apartment. A woman in a full-length silk ball gown relaxes on the sofa on a sea of cushions, next to a custom-built bed.

CHRISTINE *stands in the mess of a room, next to the TV (music and test card), looking at a copy of* Homes and Gardens.

A key goes into and turns in the front door lock. CHRISTINE *slams off the TV, hides behind the sofa.* ROSE *lets herself into the flat.* CHRISTINE *jumps out – brings* ROSE *to the floor with a rugger tackle.*

>   CHRISTINE
> Gotcha!

They roll around on the floor.

>   CHRISTINE
> Where's my bloody rent?

They fight. ROSE *tries to escape into the hall but* CHRISTINE *clings to her legs.*

Loud banging on the front door.

>   CHRISTINE
> Aahh!

>   MAN'S VOICE
>   (outside)
> Miss Painter!

Panic. CHRISTINE *and* ROSE *crawl in circles, wedge themselves against the front door, beneath the letter-box.*

>   MAN'S VOICE
> Miss Painter!

>   CHRISTINE
>   (whispers to Rose)
> Rent! You owe me rent!

>   ROSE
> Shhh!

THE MAN *raps hard on the door. The letter-box slams open. The black moustache and mouth of* MR PILKINGTON, *the landlord, appear as he shouts through the gap.*

>   MR PILKINGTON
> Miss Painter! I know you're in there! Open up!

CHRISTINE
(to Rose)
I want my rent!

ROSE *whines and complains about most things. (And she suffers from poor circulation, her hands and feet are always cold.)*

MR PILKINGTON
I want my rent — you hear me? R-E-N-T spells rent. I know you're in there.

CHRISTINE *and* ROSE *begin to see the funny side of the situation, they are just inches away from* MR PILKINGTON. CHRISTINE *sticks out her tongue and gives him the V sign.* ROSE *lifts her skirt and points to her knickers.*

MR PILKINGTON
(can't see them)
Rent by Friday or I send in the heavy mob, see how you like it!

The letter-box slams shut. Relief. CHRISTINE *and* ROSE *slumped on the floor.*

ROSE
Oh, Gawd, I'm sorry, Christine. I ain't done the business. I've had the curse. And the 'flu. Terrible 'flu and the curse as well. I'm here all on my own. And the baby to look after. Business is terrible.

ROSE *goes into the bedroom and begins to unplug the TV.*

CHRISTINE
Then get a maid.

ROSE
There's the door to answer, the phone, the client to service. I can't do it all, can I?

ROSE *picks up the TV, portable aerial balanced on top.*

ROSE
I gotta go before someone steals the baby.

CHRISTINE
What are you doing with that?

ROSE
(pathetic)
My one's broke.

CHRISTINE
I'll get you one.

ROSE
A telly?

CHRISTINE
A maid!

ROSE
You?

CHRISTINE
First thing Monday morning. There'll be one here. Get
your knickers into gear.

| 14 | INT. | MANSION BLOCK | DAY |

*A large Victorian mansion block, considerably up-market from anything we've
seen so far. A large, open staircase, polished banisters, with an open cage lift
running up the centre of the stairwell.*

*CHRISTINE, alone, is in the lift. CAMERA follows the lift's progress to
the second floor. The lift doors echo open. CHRISTINE walks along the
carpeted corridor, takes out the bunch of keys and opens the front door into:*

| 15 | INT. | THE APARTMENT | DAY |

*A large, open apartment. Deserted. CHRISTINE turns on the lights in the
bedroom. A large room, everything in pinks, lots of satins, worn and faded. A
large bed. A large sofa and built-in wardrobes with full-length mirrors. There
are some sex magazines on a bedside cabinet. Everything is tidy.*

She removes her coat, she is still wearing her waitress's uniform.

*CHRISTINE opens a large drawer full of frilly underwear of different colours:
peek-a-boo bras, suspenders, split-crotch panties, etc. CHRISTINE takes out
a pair of the panties, inspects them, puts her hand through the hole in the split
crotch.*

*The front doorbell rings. CHRISTINE walks out of the bedroom, along the
hallway to the front door, opens it, just a little. On the other side of the door is
MR MARSDEN (early fifties).*

CHRISTINE
Yes?

MR MARSDEN
Er ... is Melanie here?

CHRISTINE
No, she's not.

*She closes the door in MR MARSDEN's face and walks back along the hall
towards the bedroom. Another ring at the front doorbell. She goes back to the
door and opens it.*

MR MARSDEN
Er ... are you free at the moment?

CHRISTINE
Are you a married man?

MR MARSDEN
Yes.

CHRISTINE
What about your wife then, what's wrong with her?

MR MARSDEN
We've not had sex for the past twenty-three years. Are you available?

CHRISTINE
(insulted)
What do you think I am?

She slams the door in his face. She stands at the door for some moments, thinking about the incident. Once again, she walks back along the hall towards the bedroom. Yet another ring at the front doorbell, slightly more insistent. She goes back to the door – had enough of this game – pulls it open expecting to find Mr Marsden. Instead, she finds:

CHRISTINE
Mr Popozogolou.

MR POPOZOGOLOU
Miss Painter. How convenient to find you at home. May I come in?

CHRISTINE
(no choice)
Yes, come in.

MR POPOZOGOLOU *(58) is a modest, polite man with sad eyes and a black moustache. He is the landlord. He follows* CHRISTINE *along the hall towards the lounge, the curtains are closed.*

CHRISTINE
Come in, take a seat . . . oh.

She turns on the light – chaos. Empty bottles and glasses, girlie magazines lying around, full ash trays. A standard lamp has fallen on to the sofa. She quickly turns off the light.

CHRISTINE
Oh! This way. In here.

She takes him to the bedroom.

MR POPOZOGOLOU
(having glimpsed the room)
You been having a party?

CHRISTINE *holds open the bedroom door.*

>**CHRISTINE**
>Come in, sit down, make yourself at home.

MR POPOZOGOLOU *looks round the pink bedroom. His sad eyes rest on the open drawer of underwear and on a red négligé lying over the back of a chair.*

CHRISTINE *tries to smile at* MR POPOZOGOLOU *who, turning away from the underwear, takes out a small account book from his inside pocket.*

>**CHRISTINE**
>I expect you're here for the rent.

>**MR POPOZOGOLOU**
>That is correct, yes.

MR POPOZOGOLOU *looks at the column of figures in the book, as if he didn't already know the sums written down.*

CHRISTINE *nervous, sits on the long sofa.*

>**MR POPOZOGOLOU**
>Miss Painter, you are one week behind with your rent. One whole week.

MR POPOZOGOLOU, *sad and sympathetic, stares at* CHRISTINE.

>**CHRISTINE**
>I haven't got it — but I can get it. I always pay my way. I believe in paying my own way.

MR POPOZOGOLOU *looks at* CHRISTINE *as she sits on the long sofa.*

>**MR POPOZOGOLOU**
>That is very correct.

MR POPOZOGOLOU *taps his notebook, closes it, sits on the sofa next to* CHRISTINE. *Deferential.*

>**MR POPOZOGOLOU**
>You don't live here, do you?

>**CHRISTINE**
>I'd like to live here.

>**MR POPOZOGOLOU**
>You are sub-letting, yes?

>**CHRISTINE**
>I suppose so.

>**MR POPOZOGOLOU**
>(sighs)
>To what kind of person you are sub-letting?

CHRISTINE
The same as a lot of the other flats in this block. You should know.

MR POPOZOGOLOU
Prostitutes?

CHRISTINE
Tarts.

MR POPOZOGOLOU
I see.

CHRISTINE
You're doing all right here. All these flats. What a racket.

MR POPOZOGOLOU
Miss Painter, what are you going to do about the rent?

CHRISTINE
I've got a son at school, private school, I have to pay the fees. I'll give it you next week.

MR POPOZOGOLOU
Why wait until next week?

CHRISTINE
Give me a week.

MR POPOZOGOLOU
Why wait until next week when you can pay me now?

Quite a long pause. CHRISTINE *stares at* MR POPOZOGOLOU.

CHRISTINE
I ... can't pay you now. . . .

MR POPOZOGOLOU
The rent, Miss Painter, it must be paid. One way or another.

CHRISTINE
(a slow dawning awareness)
Oh.

MR POPOZOGOLOU, *sad and sympathetic, makes no move.*

16   EXT.   THE NEW VICTORIA CAFE

Early evening/tea time.

A slack time, not many customers in the café. A different waitress, ANGELA *(16), serves at the tables, helped out by* BENITO, *the manager.*

CHRISTINE, SHIRLEY *and* DOLLY *sit together at one of the tables drinking tea and eating snacks. There are some woman's magazines on the table – Woman's Realm, Woman etc. – and* CHRISTINE's *copy of* Homes and Gardens. CHRISTINE *and* DOLLY *swap magazines, a casual ritual.*

CHRISTINE *is more than a little preoccupied with the events of the day.*

On the other side of the street, a MAN *peers through a theodolite, surveying the road. He is handsome, well dressed, casual and relaxed.* CHRISTINE *watches him as he works, but without consciously taking him in.*

> CHRISTINE
> I had a sexual encounter with my landlord today.
>
> SHIRLEY
> What brought that on?
>
> CHRISTINE
> The rent. Mr Popozogolou.

DOLLY *snorts, almost laughs.*

CHRISTINE
That's his name, silly bugger.

SHIRLEY
Christine, get rid of them.

CHRISTINE
What?

SHIRLEY
Those flats. Get rid of them, all of them.

DOLLY
She's right, Christine.

CHRISTINE
If the cows paid the rent.

SHIRLEY
They won't pay the rent.

CHRISTINE
You're the only ones that pay.

SHIRLEY
Bugger the girls, get rid of the flats.

CHRISTINE *grabs the* Homes and Gardens *from* DOLLY. *She shows them the picture of the luxurious apartment.*

CHRISTINE
Dolly, Dolly, look at this, isn't it lovely? I could live in that.

As DOLLY *looks at the picture,* CHRISTINE *glances at* THE MAN *working with the theodolite.*

SHIRLEY
Here.

SHIRLEY *gives* CHRISTINE *some money.*

CHRISTINE
What's this for?

SHIRLEY
A bit extra.

CHRISTINE
You've already paid. You can't pay twice.

SHIRLEY
We've been using the living-room and the bedroom.

DOLLY
We've been off our feet.

SHIRLEY
And I'm away the next two weeks.

A blow for CHRISTINE – *she had forgotten this.*

> CHRISTINE
> Is that next week?

> SHIRLEY
> The next two weeks. I told you. I'm in Saudi Arabia this
> weekend, then off down to Ron's mum in Brighton.
> (to Dolly)
> Go now, don't have to do it at Christmas.

> DOLLY
> Mm.

> CHRISTINE
> (astonished)
> Saudi Arabia . . .?

> SHIRLEY
> For the weekend.

> CHRISTINE
> For the weekend?

She looks to DOLLY *for confirmation.*

> DOLLY
> She's got a sheikh in Saudi Arabia.

CHRISTINE *is fantastically impressed.*

> SHIRLEY
> A hundred and four if he's a day. Flies me out when he gets
> randy.

> DOLLY
> Once every two years.

> SHIRLEY
> What about your sugar daddy, him in the big car? He's got
> loads of money – what's his name?

> CHRISTINE
> Sydney.

> SHIRLEY
> Sydney –

> DOLLY
> (almost smiles)
> BCSD.

> CHRISTINE
> (confirms this)
> BCSD.

SHIRLEY
What's BCSD?

DOLLY
Big car, small dick.

CHRISTINE
It's true, Shirley, I can't find it. I spend all me time
rummaging inside his pyjamas trying to find his little
willy. It's hopeless. There's too many things can go wrong
with sex. Too many bits and pieces.

DOLLY
He takes you to nice places.

CHRISTINE
(shakes her head)
There's no romance.

SHIRLEY
No dick.

CHRISTINE
No dick.

They laugh – attracting attention from other CUSTOMERS.

CHRISTINE
Not like Mr Popozogolou. He had a really funny one, did
Mr Popozogolou.

SHIRLEY
Marry him – keep you laughing.

CHRISTINE
It was like – it wasn't long, but, my God, it was . . . like . . .
what are they called? Those German sausages?

SHIRLEY
Salamis.

DOLLY
Liverwurst.

CHRISTINE
Liverwurst! It was like a lump of liverwurst.

Laughter, they're enjoying themselves now.

CHRISTINE
(indicates a really thick penis)
Like that. Ugh! He wanted me to put it in his mouth. Can
you imagine?

DOLLY
His mouth?

CHRISTINE
(corrects herself)
My mouth. He wanted me to . . . you know . . .
(opens her mouth, indicates with her finger, still
laughing)
Aaahhh . . . you know?

SHIRLEY
What did you do?

CHRISTINE
I went down and had a look.

SHIRLEY
Then what?

CHRISTINE
Came back up again. Bloody quick, I can tell you. Ugh! I
can't do it for love, let alone money.

SHIRLEY
So what did you do?

CHRISTINE
I did him with my hand. This one.

SHIRLEY
A hand job.

CHRISTINE
That's right.

SHIRLEY
A wank.

DOLLY
A Popozogolou.

CHRISTINE and SHIRLEY *laugh*, DOLLY *keeps a straight face.*

CHRISTINE
A Popozogolou! It went —
(indicates the parabola of the sperm)
Brup! Like that. Brup! Really high. Even he was surprised.
If I'd have, you know, had me tonsils round that . . .

CHRISTINE *breaks up into hysterical laughter, covers her mouth.*

SHIRLEY *gets up to go to the counter to pay for the teas and snacks.*

SHIRLEY
I'll pay.

DOLLY
I need a wee.

SHIRLEY *goes to the counter.* CHRISTINE *and* DOLLY *collect up their things and head for the exit.*

CHRISTINE
(reflects)
He's a nice man, Mr Popozogolou, I felt sorry for him.
(to Dolly)
What are you going to do the next two weeks?

DOLLY
I thought I'd knit a cardie.

CHRISTINE
You know Rose?

DOLLY
Scrag-end Rose?

CHRISTINE
Could you maid for her — just for a few days, until she finds someone else?

DOLLY *shakes her head.*

> DOLLY
> No.

> CHRISTINE
> Why not?

> DOLLY
> She's a scrubber. I wouldn't maid for no scrubber.

From inside the café, we see CHRISTINE, SHIRLEY *and* DOLLY *walk out of the New Victoria.*

SHIRLEY *is met by* RON, *her husband.* RON *is a mild-mannered bloke, he usually has a roll-up cigarette in his mouth.*

RON *gives* SHIRLEY *a peck on the cheek and opens the door of their car (a Ford Cortina) for* SHIRLEY *as she gets in.*

DOLLY *and* CHRISTINE *walk off in opposite directions.*

---

17   INT.   BATHROOM/CHRISTINE'S FLAT   NIGHT

MUSIC: Pepe Jaramillo and His Latin American Rhythm play 'Romantica Madalena Samba'.

P.O.V. along the hall of the now familiar poster of Charles and Diana into: CHRISTINE *wearing a bath hat, in the bath. On the bathroom wall above her head, a full colour poster of the Doris Day movie* Lullaby of Broadway.

CHRISTINE *reflects on the events of the day.*

---

18   INT.   BEDROOM/CHRISTINE'S FLAT   NIGHT

Light spills from the hall into the bedroom. CHRISTINE, *wrapped in the towel and still wearing her bath hat, walks over and sits on the end of her single bed. Deeply preoccupied, she dries between her toes. She turns on the bedside light, returns to drying her toes, then . . .*

. . . from within the bed, something stirs. A violent shock. CHRISTINE *screams and catapults back to the other side of the room.*

Equally startled, a bizarre figure sits bolt upright in CHRISTINE's *bed. Fully grown adult male, clutching a toy doll and wearing a large frilled blue satin mob cap; a blue satin nightgown (also with many frills); and (under the covers) nylon stockings, blue satin baby boots and a nappy. Sticking out of this giant* BABY's *mouth is a giant, pink baby's dummy.*

Both are equally terrified of the other. Each time one moves the other jumps and screams.

THE BABY
(removing the dummy)
I —

CHRISTINE
(very fast)
What is it what is it what are you doing what are you
doing?!

THE BABY
(Scots accent)
Nobody woke me.

CHRISTINE
What are you doing?

THE BABY
It's hell at work these days . . .

The phone rings, violently startling both CHRISTINE *and* THE BABY.
THE BABY *leaps up and stands on the bed.* CHRISTINE *screams and
lunges for the telephone receiver.*

CHRISTINE
(screeches)
Hello! Shirley! Ahh! Yes. Yes. It's here, it's here. It just —
it's right here.
(hesitates)
You're sure?

THE BABY
(looks at his watch)
Oh God, will you look at the time — my wife'll wonder
where the hell I've been . . .

CHRISTINE
I believe you, Shirley, I believe you . . .
Mr Who?

The doorbell rings, sending more shock waves through CHRISTINE. *She
drops the telephone.*

CHRISTINE
Ah!

THE BABY
Please . . .

CHRISTINE *backs towards the door.*

CHRISTINE
(as she goes)
It's all right, Mr MacLehone . . .

> THE BABY
> (corrects her)
> McCellan.

CHRISTINE *backs out into the hall and opens the front door where she finds* SYDNEY (BCSD), *all dressed for the Dorchester, and smoking a large cigar.*

> SYDNEY
> Come on, babe, chop chop, put on your frock.

CHRISTINE *just stares at him.*

> CHRISTINE
> Babe?

> SYDNEY
> (puts on a Yankee accent)
> Yeah, sure, come on, babe, Daddy's taking you out.

> CHRISTINE
> Daddy wants a baby?
> (grabs him)
> You want a baby, Daddy? Here. One Daddy. One baby.

She shoves SYDNEY *into the bedroom, retreats into the bathroom and locks the door.*

> CHRISTINE
> Oh God.

In the bedroom: SYDNEY *confronts* THE BABY.

> THE BABY
> (on the telephone)
> I think I'd better go now, Shirley.

THE BABY *puts down the telephone receiver.*

> THE BABY
> (to Sydney)
> Hello . . . my name's Alex McCellan.

SYDNEY *does not reply.*

19   EXT.   STREET   DAY
_____

The street market and the crumbling building with the flats above.

Pick-up on TIMMS *(35) as* ROSE, *walking too fast in her very high-heel shoes, heads towards the flat, rummaging through her bag to find her keys. She is wearing a short leather jacket, a leather mini-skirt and tights. She is so cold she looks blue.*

As she goes, we hear CHRISTINE's *voice over:*

> CHRISTINE
> (shades of the speaking clock)
> That is correct, yes. She is a young model of twenty-one. A
> petite figure but very sexy. You will like her.

ROSE *walks up the outside staircase — now clean and tidy — to the front door of the flat.*

> CHRISTINE
> (continuing)
> She offers a full personal service, sophisticated, discreet
> and clean. Five o'clock last caller. Why not pop round?

ROSE *fumbles to get the key into the lock; she's so cold, her hands are shaking.*

> CHRISTINE
> We are thirty-three, that's three-a-three Pierpoint Street.
> That's right, as in Albert.

20   INT.   ROSE'S FLAT   DAY

ROSE *walks into the flat as* CHRISTINE *hangs up the phone.*

> ROSE
> Oh, God, I'm cold! Bloody buses. I'm freezing. What man in
> his right mind wants to get his cock out in this weather?

> CHRISTINE
> Hope to see you then. Bye.

She stops, hesitates, taking in CHRISTINE *for the first time. The flat is looking much cleaner and tidier, but could never be home.*

CHRISTINE *is wearing an apron and carpet slippers. She signals to* ROSE *to lower her voice and points towards the living-room.*

> ROSE
> What are you doing here?

> CHRISTINE
> Sshh! We've got one.

> ROSE
> What?

> CHRISTINE
> A client. I'm your new maid.

> ROSE
> You? A prostitute's maid?

> CHRISTINE
> Why not? Get a move on, we've got a client.

> ROSE
> Bugger him, he'll have to wait. I need a coffee.

ROSE *heads for the kitchen,* CHRISTINE *jams her against the door post.*

> CHRISTINE
> You listen to me. I've chucked my job at the café for this —
> so get in there, get on your back and get busy.

> ROSE
> (slightly intimidated)
> Who is it? I don't want no time wasters.

ROSE *goes into the living-room to view the client — a* MR DUNKLEY, *a polite gentleman in his mid-fifties.*

> ROSE
> (recognises him)
> Oh, it's you. All right, I'll do you first. Come on.

MR DUNKLEY *has already had a coffee. He hands the empty cup to* CHRISTINE.

> MR DUNKLEY
> Thank you.

CHRISTINE *watches as* MR DUNKLEY *follows* ROSE *into the bedroom. Bang. The bedroom door closes, concealing God knows what.*

CHRISTINE *grabs the Ewbank handsweeper and begins to sweep the floor, loitering near the bedroom. She proceeds to spray the room with 'Springtime Bouquet' from an aerosol can.*

She kneels down to try to get a view through the key-hole — spraying as she goes.

The bedroom door opens. CHRISTINE *reels backwards and goes berserk with the 'Springtime Bouquet'.*

> ROSE
> (smelling the spray)
> Bloody hell.

> CHRISTINE
> That was quick.

> ROSE
> See the man to the door then.

> CHRISTINE
> (stunned by the brevity of the encounter)
> Yes. Yes, of course.

> MR DUNKLEY
> Goodbye. Thank you.

MR DUNKLEY *slips a pound note (a tip) into* CHRISTINE's *hand.*

CHRISTINE
Oh, thank you. Um . . .
(nods towards the bedroom)
Did you change your mind?

MR DUNKLEY
Pardon?

CHRISTINE
Did you change your mind?

MR DUNKLEY
No.

CHRISTINE
Oh! Ha, ha. Come again then. Nice to see you.

MR DUNKLEY
Thank you.

CHRISTINE
(closing the door)
Bye.

In the bedroom: ROSE, *bad-tempered and cold, utterly without grace, is changing into a red and black three-piece set (bra, knickers and suspenders) with black stockings and high-heels, over which she wears a 'Hollywood style full length négligé trimmed in marabou fur'. She still looks extremely cold.*

CHRISTINE
That was quick.

ROSE
(mimics)
'That was quick'. Piss off and make some coffee, will you?

CHRISTINE
You look like Dracula's daughter. No wonder trade is slack.

ROSE
(ratty)
'That was quick'.

CHRISTINE
But it was quick. It was in and out. Just like that. In – out. You look just like Dracula's daughter in that outfit, you really do.

ROSE
(loses her temper, yells at Christine)
Oh piss off, will you? Leave me alone! Just piss off.

> CHRISTINE
> Piss off yourself! This is my bloody flat. Talk to me like that. You can piss off yourself.

> ROSE
> Right.

This is just the opening ROSE has been looking for. She pulls off her négligé and stuffs it into her bag. Then puts her mini-skirt and leather jacket back on.

> ROSE
> (muttering to herself)
> Right . . . I've better things to do . . . freezing my tits off in this dump . . . You can stick it up your gonger.

> CHRISTINE
> (hard)
> Eight weeks rent.

> ROSE
> No, no, you said piss off and piss off I shall.

> CHRISTINE
> (furious)
> Eight weeks rent!

ROSE chucks the keys to CHRISTINE, hitting her in the middle of the chest, and is on her way out of the front door.

> ROSE
> Here! You reckon you're so bloody juicy, get on your back and earn it yourself. Cow!

ROSE slams the front door, leaving CHRISTINE standing in the hall — stunned.

The phone rings. It rings for quite some time before she answers it.

> CHRISTINE
> Hello . . . No, she's not here . . . no . . . She's . . . she's gone to a health farm . . . yes . . . but if you ring tomorrow there'll be a new girl on.

She hangs up.

---

21   EXT.   TOBACCONIST'S SHOP   DAY

CHRISTINE stands outside a tobacconist's shop on the opposite side of the road to the New Victoria café.

In the window, an extraordinary and rich selection of notices catering for those with an interest in the purchase of sexual events:

'Dominant Ex-Governess seeks afternoon pupils. Ring . . .'

The card next to it reads:

'French Polishing a Speciality'.

And more:

'Large Chest For Sale'

'Swedish Massage by Helga'

'Wicker Seats Re-Caned'

'Madam Sasha – Expert in all forms of training'

'Construction and Demolition – By Appointment Only'

'Games Mistress'

'Have Cane – Will Travel'

'O-Level Students Invited and Encouraged'

'My Pee-Wee is like a nectar to thee
So I demand You come to Me'

. . . and so on. All with phone numbers.

CHRISTINE *studies the notices for some time, then turns, walks to the pavement edge to look across the road to the New Victoria – almost bumping into* THE MAN, *the surveyor, as she goes. He notices her, but she does not notice him.*

Inside the café CHRISTINE *can see her friends,* JACKIE *and* JUNE, *busy with the lunchtime rush. All she has to do is cross the road – and she's back in the catering business. She watches, preoccupied, on the outside looking in.*

CHRISTINE *turns and moves on, away from the New Victoria café.*

| 22 | INT. | BEDROOM/CHRISTINE'S FLAT | NIGHT |

CHRISTINE *snaps a black suspender on to a black stocking and looks at herself in the wardrobe mirror.*

She is wearing a nylon tiger print camisole, 'the fitted bodice gives a perfect shape and features a button-up front and detachable suspenders'. With this, a black lace choker, black stockings and rollers in her hair.

She stands on her toes to simulate high-heels and studies her reflection.

CHRISTINE *contemplates the effect – which is not all she had hoped for.*

> CHRISTINE
> (sighs)
> Dracula's daughter.

She returns to a plate of cold baked beans on toast. Propped in front of the plate, the copy of Homes and Gardens. *A woman sits in opulent splendour. Headline: 'A Woman's Place is in the Home'.*

MUSIC and MIX to:

| 23 | INT. | LIFT/MANSION BLOCK | NIGHT |

Inside the metal cage lift in the mansion block.

CHRISTINE's *white gloved hand presses the button to floor number 2. The lift indicator shows the progression of the lift . . . floor 1 . . . 2 . . . 3 . . .*

CHRISTINE's *white gloved hand again presses the second floor button. No effect. The lift continues, up and up.*

Floor 6 . . . 7 . . . 8 . . . 9 . . .

The number of floors in the apartment block seems to have dramatically increased.

Floor 15 . . . 16 . . . 17 . . . onwards and upwards . . . 23 . . . 24 . . . 25 . . . and the lift stops. The indicator on the lift flashes the words 'Penthouse Suite'.

The lift doors open and CHRISTINE *steps out. She is in a full-length ball gown, echoes of Hartnell, a stunner as worn by the model in* Homes and Gardens.

She has stepped out of the lift into the real-life dream world apartment in the clouds of Homes and Gardens, *space and luxury beyond the rampant materialist's wildest aspirations.*

First she sees the theodolite. Then THE MAN. *Suave and immaculate, dressed in bow tie and evening suit, the perfect gentleman, he pours champagne into two glasses as he steps forwards and kisses* CHRISTINE.

After the kiss, warm and tender, he gives her a glass of champagne. They drink. He leads her to a sofa, a mile long, drenched in cushions, and one of many. Through large double-doors we glimpse the bedroom: real silks and satins, subtle blends of colours. This is Homes and Gardens *at its very best. Huge plate glass windows open out on to panoramic views of a sleeping city lit by moonlight.*

CHRISTINE *and her* MAN *sit together on the sofa, close. He gives her a gardenia.*

They kiss again and drink champagne. Pure romance.

CHRISTINE *dissolves into a warm and sticky ecstasy as* THE MAN *slides a Bravington's engagement ring on to her finger.*

They are about to kiss when the doorbell rings, loud and insistent. They hesitate:

24   INT.   HALL/CHRISTINE'S FLAT   NIGHT

Darkness.

CHRISTINE *staggers out of her bedroom, puts on the hall light, and lunges towards the front door. She is in her nightdress, 97% asleep, hair in rollers.*

She opens the front door to find SYDNEY, *in evening dress, with cigar as usual, holding a large bunch of flowers (at least 2½ dozen red roses), a bottle of champagne and two glasses. He is in a somewhat serious and pensive mood.*

> SYDNEY
> Hello, babe, can I come in, babe?

> CHRISTINE
> Oh, God, Sydney, do I need it?

CHRISTINE *treks back along the hall followed by* SYDNEY, *into the bedroom and gets into bed.*

> CHRISTINE
> What do you want, Sydney? It's the middle of the night, what do you want?

> SYDNEY
> (serious, worried, sits on the end of the bed)
> Oh, babe, I've been thinking, babe.

> CHRISTINE
> I'm not a babe, Sydney. I'm not your babe or anybody's baby, all right?

> SYDNEY
> (innocent)
> I know you're not, babe.

CHRISTINE *sighs, closes her eyes.*

> CHRISTINE
> What do you want?

> SYDNEY
> I've come to ask you to marry me.

CHRISTINE *groans and puts her hands over her eyes.*

> SYDNEY
> I know it's not a very good idea, babe, I know it's not, but if you think about it, it is.

CHRISTINE *sighs, eyes still closed.*

> SYDNEY
> You need somebody. You need somebody to look after you.
> I've got loads of money, you know, loads of it, no one to
> share it with. I could look after you.

A long pause. CHRISTINE *does not open her eyes.*

> SYDNEY
> Say 'yes' and I'll open the bottle right now. Pop. Just like
> that. A bottle of bubbly.

Another pause. CHRISTINE *does not respond.*

> SYDNEY
> I brought you some flowers. You think about it, babe.
> When you wake in the morning and see these flowers, you
> think about it. There's a bottle of bubbly waiting.

Long pause. CHRISTINE *does not open her eyes. She is willing herself
asleep.*

SYDNEY *puts the flowers on the bedside cabinet.*

> SYDNEY
> There.

SYDNEY *turns and walks out of the bedroom, not looking back.*

---

25   EXT.   CHRISTINE'S FLAT   DAY
_____

CHRISTINE, *looking smart and business-like, walks briskly out of the front
door. She is carrying the bunch of 2½ dozen red roses.*

*She stops to check something in her handbag. She takes out a card. On it is
written: 'To our future, babe – Sydney.' She turns it over. On the reverse is
written 'FRENCH POLISHING – put yourself in the hands of an expert –
Ring . . .'*

She walks off down the road.

---

26   EXT.   TOBACCONIST'S SHOP   DAY
_____

*Shot of the ad-cards in the shop window. CAMERA moves in on Christine's
card:*

'FRENCH POLISHING etc. . .'

MR MARSDEN *studies the notice board and notes the number of this
particular advertisement before moving on.*

DOLLY *raps on the lavatory door.*

> DOLLY
> One on the way, dear.

> CHRISTINE
> (in the lav)
> One on the way. Ha, ha. I hope not.

CHRISTINE *comes out of the lavatory.*

> CHRISTINE
> Dolly, I can't stop piddling. Where's the gin?

She pours herself a slug of gin from a half bottle. Shades of '61 in her rather sensible two-piece, Dralon/cotton, drip-dry outfit.

> DOLLY
> You don't have to do it, you know, not if you don't want to.

> CHRISTINE
> What's sex ever done for me? Up the duff at sixteen, that's me, dear.

> DOLLY
> That's no reason. If you don't want to do it, don't.

Doorbell. CHRISTINE *leaps, spills her gin.*

> CHRISTINE
> Aah!

DOLLY *catches her on the recoil.* CHRISTINE *giggles, sees the ridiculous side of it.*

> DOLLY
> Pull yourself together, do. Get in there, go on.

Into the living-room, heading towards the bedroom.

> CHRISTINE
> God, I need another widdle. How much do I charge?

> DOLLY
> I'll deal with that, go on.

In the bedroom;

In a jug, on the table, Sydney's 2½ dozen red roses. On the bed, the tiger print camisole and knickers.

CHRISTINE *grabs the camisole and knickers, intending to hide them, then changes her mind. Instead of hiding the lingerie, she lays it out on the bed. She is fully dressed, but her underwear is there to see.*

DOLLY
(head round the door)
Ready dear?

CHRISTINE
I'm ready.

DOLLY
You don't look it.

CHRISTINE
I'm ready!

DOLLY *ushers* MR MARSDEN *into the room. Moment of recognition.*

CHRISTINE
Oh! Ooh! It's you! Fancy meeting you here.

CHRISTINE *thinks it's hilarious, tries not to show it, but with not much success.*

MR MARSDEN
(to Dolly)
We know each other.

CHRISTINE
(ushers him in)
Come in, come in. It's all right, Dolly. Shut your mouth, go on, it's all right.

She hustles DOLLY *out of the room.*

CHRISTINE
(repeats her joke)
Well, fancy meeting you here.

MR MARSDEN
Caught up with you at last, eh?

MR MARSDEN *notices the lingerie on the bed.* CHRISTINE *catches his reaction.* MR MARSDEN *is always polite, never salacious.*

CHRISTINE
Would you like a cup of tea?

MR MARSDEN
(still backtracking)
Pardon?

CHRISTINE
Would you like a cup of tea?

MR MARSDEN *looks at his watch, not sure if he's in a café or a brothel.*

MR MARSDEN
Well —

CHRISTINE
Have two. No extra charge.
(she laughs)

MR MARSDEN
(still looking at his watch)
— I've only got a short time.

CHRISTINE
(takes it personally)
Oh.

MR MARSDEN
Business.

CHRISTINE
What line of business are you in?

MR MARSDEN
Double-glazing.

MR MARSDEN *looks at the knickers on the bed, his imagination runs ahead.*

CHRISTINE
(watches his reaction)
Double-glazing! Well, I never.

MR MARSDEN
(thinks about double-glazing)
Yes.

CHRISTINE
What a lot of job satisfaction there must be — in double-glazing — bringing all that extra warmth into people's lives. You've not had sex for twenty-three years, have you?

MR MARSDEN
Pardon?

CHRISTINE
You told me.

MR MARSDEN
(catches on)
No, with my wife. I've not had sex with my wife for twenty-three years.

CHRISTINE
Oh!

MR MARSDEN
She's an invalid.

CHRISTINE
(thinking of him, *not* Mrs Marsden)
I am sorry, twenty-three years, it must get very
frustrating for you.

Eyes meet – is this the moment?

MR MARSDEN
Your maid said you give excellent French.

CHRISTINE
Oh, yes, very good, every time.

*(At this point, it must be said that CHRISTINE has not the faintest notion of
what 'French' is.)*

MR MARSDEN
Good.

CHRISTINE
Just exactly how do you like your French?

MR MARSDEN
(looking towards the lingerie)
I'd like you to wear bright red lipstick, if you can –

CHRISTINE
Really?

MR MARSDEN
I'm willing to pay extra for that.

CHRISTINE
(very puzzled)
Right. Bright red lips . . .
(suddenly thinks of something)
Oh! Ah! Ooh! Oh, no. Just a minute.

CHRISTINE *nips out of the bedroom into the living-room.* DOLLY *is
knitting the cardie, now well advanced, and reading* People's Friend.

CHRISTINE *scrambles around in a drawer, looking for a stick of Rose's old
lipstick.*

CHRISTINE
Dolly! Dolly, we got no doo-dahs! No – you know –
contraventives.

DOLLY *looks at her, she doesn't know.*

DOLLY
Contraventives?

CHRISTINE *has found the lipstick and is putting it on – garish red lips.*

> CHRISTINE
> (demonstrates)
> Yes ... you know. Doo-dahs!

> DOLLY
> French letters.

> CHRISTINE
> That's it. Plonkers. We got no plonkers, Dolly.

DOLLY *rummages in her bag, down beneath the knitting wool, and produces several packets of contraceptives.*

CHRISTINE *studies the effect of the lipstick.*

> CHRISTINE
> Look a right bloody tart in this.

> DOLLY
> (gives her a couple of packets)
> Here. Get a move on.

CHRISTINE *takes them and heads back towards the bedroom, checking out the contraceptives as she goes.*

> CHRISTINE
> These are black! Dolly, these are black!

> DOLLY
> I know.

> CHRISTINE
> They're for black men, aren't they?

> DOLLY
> No, Chinamen use them all the time.

> CHRISTINE
> (surprised and interested)
> Do they?
> (heads for the bedroom)
> Bloody Ada! He's a lovely man. Brings happiness to millions with double-glazing.
> (whispers)
> He's not had sex for twenty-three years.

CHRISTINE *runs back into the bedroom and shuts the door as the phone rings.*

CHRISTINE *sits on the bed, points to the lipstick.*

> CHRISTINE
> Right. Do you think this looks nice?

> MR MARSDEN
> Oh, yes ... I'd prefer it in a chair, if you don't mind.

CHRISTINE
In a chair . . .?

MR MARSDEN
Yes.

CHRISTINE *gets a chair.*

CHRISTINE
I've never done it in a chair. How would you like me
exactly?

MR MARSDEN
Well, with me, myself, sitting. And you kneeling.

CHRISTINE *looks at the chair, tries to work it out: how is intercourse
possible in this position?*

CHRISTINE
You want me to sit?

MR MARSDEN
No, me to sit.

CHRISTINE
Where am I?

MR MARSDEN
Kneeling.

CHRISTINE
Kneeling?

MR MARSDEN
Yes, I'm sitting and you're kneeling, on the floor.

CHRISTINE
On the floor?

MR MARSDEN
I find that's the best way.

CHRISTINE
(still totally confused)
I see. Well, you'll have to wear one of these.

She holds up a contraceptive

MR MARSDEN
For French?

CHRISTINE
For anything. Do you think I want to get pregnant?

MR MARSDEN
How can you get pregnant?

CHRISTINE
Very easily, very easily indeed, thank you very much.

MR MARSDEN
But that's not what I want.

CHRISTINE
I should think not.

MR MARSDEN
I want —

CHRISTINE
What do you want?

MR MARSDEN
A blow job. Please. Deep throat. If possible.

CHRISTINE
Oh . . .

CHRISTINE *covers her mouth with her hand. Revelation. Gulps and swallows. Thinks of Mr Popozogolou.*

MR MARSDEN
That's why I wanted the lipstick.

CHRISTINE
(holds up the contraceptive)
You'll still have to wear one of these.

MR MARSDEN *considers for a moment, checks his watch.*

MR MARSDEN
Very well.

He turns his back, removes his jacket, shoes, then undoes his trousers.

CHRISTINE *watches this impromptu male striptease, looking for a way out of the impending blow job.*

She looks at the camisole, then begins to lift, shift up her skirt.

CHRISTINE
Do you see what I'm wearing?

MR MARSDEN *turns to look.* CHRISTINE *is wearing black suspenders, black knickers and black stockings.*

CHRISTINE
You like that, don't you?

MR MARSDEN
Yes, I do.

CHRISTINE
Do you like my legs?

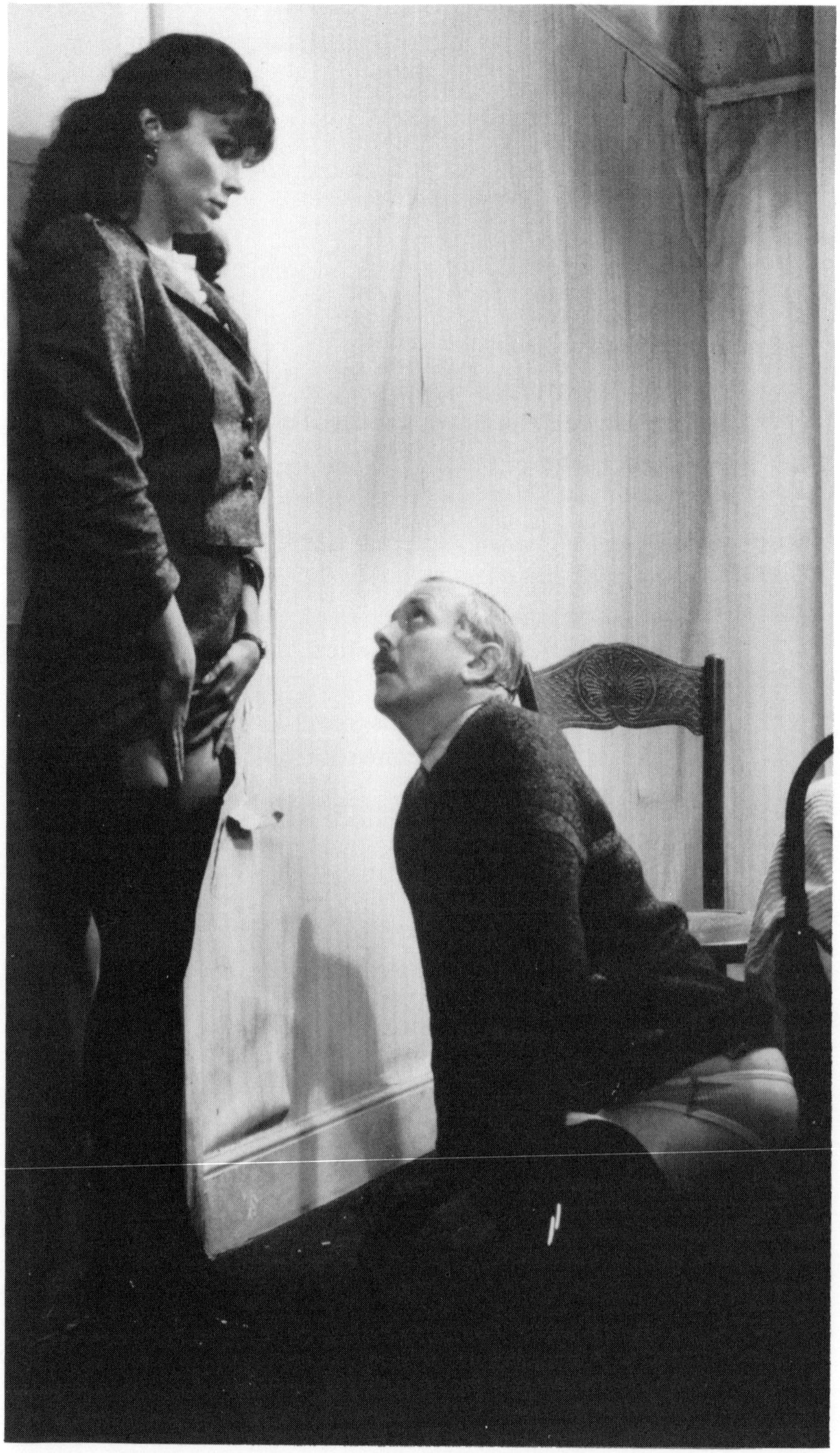

> MR MARSDEN
> Yes.

> CHRISTINE
> Do you?

> MR MARSDEN
> Yes, I do.

> CHRISTINE
> Come here, come a bit closer . . .

He does so.

> CHRISTINE
> I want you to kneel, there's a good boy, but not to touch my lovely legs.

Full of anticipation, MR MARSDEN *kneels down in front of* CHRISTINE.

> CHRISTINE
> Aren't they lovely?

> MR MARSDEN
> Yes.

> CHRISTINE
> Very smooth, just there, above the stocking, very smooth.

> MR MARSDEN
> Yes.

> CHRISTINE
> (touches the inside of her thigh)
> There. Look. Get closer . . . but not to touch. Now . . . I'm going to give you something very special, very special indeed . . . it's called . . . a Popozogolou.

CUT TO:

| 28 | INT. | THE HALL/BEDROOM/ROSE'S FLAT | DAY |

The bedroom door opens, MR MARSDEN *comes out, takes out his wallet as* DOLLY *opens the front door.*

> MR MARSDEN
> Thank you.

He slips the money into her hand.

> DOLLY
> Thank you, dear.

MR MARSDEN
She's nice, very nice indeed.

DOLLY
Good.

DOLLY *closes the front door, goes back to* CHRISTINE *in the bedroom.*

DOLLY
One here, another on the way.

CHRISTINE
Oh, bloody Ada, hang on.

CHRISTINE *sprays the room with 'Springtime Bouquet'.*

CHRISTINE
Stinks like a bleedin' brothel in here.

DOLLY
You all right?

CHRISTINE
(shakes her wrists)
Like a concert pianist, ducky. We're going to need lots of tissues.

DOLLY *turns to find* TIMMS *in the bedroom doorway, his coat done up, his hands pushed well down in his pockets.* TIMMS *is slim, looks a bit of a villain.*

DOLLY
She's not quite ready, dear.

An awkward pause. TIMMS *just stares.*

CHRISTINE
(efficient)
I'm ready. Come in, sit down, lie down, make yourself at home. Thank you, Dolly.

DOLLY *out,* CHRISTINE *closes the door.* TIMMS *looks round the room.* CHRISTINE *watches him, given half the chance, she might fancy him.*

The telephone in the hall rings.

TIMMS
You're busy.

CHRISTINE
Never a dull moment.

TIMMS
What's on offer?

CHRISTINE
Well, I've been doing French, but there's a special on today.

A Popozogolou. Very tasty. I'm sure you won't be
disappointed.

> TIMMS
> How much?

> CHRISTINE
> Dolly deals with that. Dolly deals with the lolly.

She laughs at her own joke.

> TIMMS
> Who's Dolly?

> CHRISTINE
> Her, outside. She's my maid.

> TIMMS
> Your maid. I see. And she deals with the money?

> CHRISTINE
> That's right.

TIMMS *nods his head, looks round the room, then at* CHRISTINE. *He finds
her attractive.*

> TIMMS
> (almost to himself)
> Get back to you on this one, all right?

> CHRISTINE
> Oh. Yes.

She opens the door. TIMMS *walks out of the bedroom into the living-room.*

> DOLLY
> Everything all right, dear?

> TIMMS
> I discuss the price with you, right?

> DOLLY
> If you want, yes.

> TIMMS
> Good. See you later.

TIMMS *leaves.*

> CHRISTINE
> Funny man.

> DOLLY
> Gangster.

> CHRISTINE
> Sexy bugger.

As TIMMS *leaves the flat, an extremely long Cadillac, glittering chrome polished to perfection and driven by an* ARAB CHAUFFEUR, *slides to a halt outside the door.*

The CHAUFFEUR *gets out, walks round the front of the car – a four-mile trek – to open the passenger door.*

Resplendent, dressed in a magnificent fur coat and dark glasses, looking like a million petro-dollars, SHIRLEY *emerges from the back of the car.*

SHIRLEY *walks into the building, attracting considerable attention from* SHOPKEEPERS *and* PASSERS-BY.

Blind as a gagged bat in her sunglasses, SHIRLEY *climbs the outside staircase. She slips, almost tumbles, has to lift her glasses to see where she's going.*

SHIRLEY *knocks on the door which is opened by* CHRISTINE.

>SHIRLEY
>Tarah!
>
>CHRISTINE
>Shirley!
>
>SHIRLEY
>Christine!
>
>CHRISTINE
>(excited)
>Dolly, Dolly, look who's here!
>
>DOLLY
>I can see.
>
>SHIRLEY
>Dolly.

SHIRLEY *and* DOLLY *kiss each other.*

>CHRISTINE
>Look! Look at the coat! Lovely! How was it? How was
>Saudi Arabia?
>
>SHIRLEY
>Cadillacs and camel shit, dear, all the way.

CHRISTINE, DOLLY *and* SHIRLEY *walk down the staircase and into the street.*

Screams of delight from CHRISTINE *when she sees the Cadillac.*

> CHRISTINE
> Oh! Look! Look at the car!
> (to the chauffeur)
> Hello!
> (to Shirley and Dolly)
> What a big one, eh? Lovely. Is it yours?

> SHIRLEY
> Taxi from the airport, dear. This is going to take me and
> my old man down to his mum's in Brighton.

> CHRISTINE
> Couple of weeks, Dolly, we'll have one of these.

> SHIRLEY
> Listen to her. What's she doing?

> DOLLY
> 'French Polishing. Put yourself in the hands of an expert.'

> SHIRLEY
> (impressed)
> French?!

> CHRISTINE
> I don't even know what it is. I don't! I just copied it off
> another notice.

> SHIRLEY
> Christine . . . french polishing —

SHIRLEY *opens her mouth, points with her finger. For* CHRISTINE, *a blinding flash of realisation.*

> CHRISTINE
> What?! Is that what it is?

SHIRLEY *nods.*

> CHRISTINE
> French polishing? Oh, my God, bloody Ada!
> (she bursts into hopeless hysterical laughter)
> Poor Mr Marsden. Better change that notice quick!

During the above, an elderly GENTLEMAN *has approached the flat, checked out the address, inspected the Cadillac, and, finally, the* THREE WOMEN.

MORTEN *(mid-sixties), a retired RAF officer, has a small pack on his back and is dressed more for a ramble in the Yorkshire Dales than a hike round the back streets of Victoria and Pimlico. There is nothing particularly 'whizzo' about his personality; since retirement after the war, he has spent most of his time working as a shopkeeper.*

WC MORTEN
Excuse me, ladies. Morten. Ex-Wing Commander, retired —

DOLLY
Oh, yes, you rang —

WC MORTEN
That is correct. I have a dilapidated piece of mahogany veneer in dire need of renovation. Can you help?

CHRISTINE
(ushers him into the door)
What? Oh, yes, we'll soon polish it up, have it looking like new in no time.

---

31   INT.   BEDROOM/FLAT ABOVE THE SHOPS   DAY

Heads and shoulders shot: CHRISTINE, EX-WING COMMANDER MORTEN *and* SHIRLEY. WC MORTEN *is in his shirt-tails. All concentration is just below the bottom of frame where the WC is getting a Popozogolou.* SHIRLEY *is there as an observer.*

CHRISTINE
Wing Commander — I don't believe a word of it.

WC MORTEN
Two hundred and seven missions over occupied territory, Madam. In bra and panties.

> **CHRISTINE**
> Shut up.
>
> **WC MORTEN**
> Yes, Madam.
>
> **CHRISTINE**
> You've got a filthy mind.
>
> **WC MORTEN**
> Yes, Madam.
>
> **SHIRLEY**
> Quite a shine on that.
>
> **WC MORTEN**
> Indeed.
>
> **SHIRLEY**
> That's coming along nicely, Auntie Christine.
>
> **CHRISTINE**
> Would you like a go?
>
> **SHIRLEY**
> No, no, you're doing nicely.
>
> **WC MORTEN**
> Why not do it together?

OUTSIDE: *the doorbell.*

> **CHRISTINE**
> You're a dirty old sod.
>
> **WC MORTEN**
> Yes, Madam, I'm certainly that, Madam –
>
> **DOLLY**
> (from outside)
> Christine!

As – bang – the bedroom door flies open. WC MORTEN *bellows in surprise. Standing in the doorway are* TIMMS *and his sidekick,* BEVIN.

Behind them, a uniformed POLICEMAN.

> **TIMMS**
> (waves a warrant)
> Police, love, you're nicked.

DOLLY *begins to cry.*

> **DOLLY**
> I'm sorry, I didn't have a chance.

CHRISTINE *looks down at the* EX-WING COMMANDER's *lap.*

CHRISTINE
(to the WC)
Pass me a tissue, Wing Commander, there's a dear.

32   INT.   COURTROOM   DAY

A corridor full of PEOPLE, *accused and accusers,* MEN *and* WOMEN, POLICEMEN *and* POLICEWOMEN, SOLICITORS, PROBATION OFFICERS, *etc., all waiting for their cases to be called.*

TIMMS *is floating around, walking up and down the corridor.*

Sitting on a bench at one end of the corridor, away from the crowd: CHRISTINE, SHIRLEY *and* DOLLY. CHRISTINE *and* DOLLY *are waiting to go into court.*

A SOLICITOR, *male, approaches them.*

During the following conversation, we pick up on four POLICEMEN – HART, WILLIAMS, BEVIN *and* BAKER. *They are watching* CHRISTINE, SHIRLEY *and* DOLLY, *generally looking them over, chuckling and whispering to each other.*

SOLICITOR
They've dropped the brothel and immoral earnings charges. Insufficient evidence.

SHIRLEY
That lets you off, Dolly.

DOLLY *tries not to react; but inside she has been relieved of a considerable burden.*

SOLICITOR
That only leaves the charge for soliciting. You'll be in and out in two minutes.

He goes.

CHRISTINE
How? How was I soliciting?

SHIRLEY
A doddle. Just plead guilty.

CHRISTINE
I was standing on the pavement looking at your Arab's motor car. I was not soliciting.

SHIRLEY
Par for the course, dear, no big thing.

DOLLY
Look at them, all these men. I know all their secrets.
That's why they want to lock us up.

SHIRLEY
Don't get deep, Dolly.

CHRISTINE
Do you think it'll be in the Harlow New Town Gazette? I
can just see my Dad's face. It's my sister's wedding
Saturday.

DOLLY
(looking at Timms)
He's a nasty little shit.

CHRISTINE
Needs a good whipping.
(suddenly to PC Hart)
What are you looking at?

HART *is a fresh-faced youth.*

CHRISTINE
You looking at my tits? He was looking at my tits. Arrest
him for looking at my tits.

The other POLICEMEN *laugh.* HART *blushes.*

CHRISTINE
He's too young to be a policeman, he's still a virgin.

More laughs from the POLICEMEN.

PC BAKER *strolls over, he's a big bloke.*

BAKER
I bet you could change all that.

COURT USHER
(calls)
Painter. Painter, please.

CHRISTINE
(stands. To Baker)
Drive a car?

BAKER
Yeah.

CHRISTINE
Drive a big car, do you?

BAKER
Yeah.

CHRISTINE
(looks to Shirley and Dolly)
Thought so.

SHIRLEY *and* DOLLY *laugh. The* SOLICITOR *approaches.*

SOLICITOR
Right, we're on.

CHRISTINE *has gained some confidence.*

CHRISTINE
Right. Guilty. I'm guilty. It's all my fault.

She walks towards the courtroom with the SOLICITOR *just as* TIMMS
opens the courtroom door.

CHRISTINE
Thank you.

She strides into court, leaving TIMMS *to follow on behind just as* WC
MORTEN *arrives, somewhat out of breath. He's wearing a suit, well cared
for, but advanced in years.*

WC MORTEN
What news, ladies?

SHIRLEY
What are you doing here?

WC MORTEN
Interested party, character witness. Has she gone in?

SHIRLEY
Just put your bum down there.

WC MORTEN
Thank you.

RON *shows up, winks at* SHIRLEY *and* DOLLY, *gives the* POLICE-
MEN *the cold eye.*

SHIRLEY
(to Ron)
Hello, love.

DOLLY
She'll need a holiday after this lot.

SHIRLEY
She's very good, you know. She's got talent.

WC MORTEN
That is correct.

DOLLY
How do you know?

> **WC MORTEN**
> I am an expert in these matters.

> **SHIRLEY**
> (to Dolly)
> We should go in together. The three of us. Take that big flat of hers, the one with the pink bedroom. Cater for kinks. Strictly for kinky people.

> **WC MORTEN**
> The future lies in kinky people.

TIMMS *comes out of the courtroom, a smile to* SHIRLEY *and* DOLLY, *then joins* BEVIN *near the exit. Then* CHRISTINE, *looking definitely pleased with herself.*

WC MORTEN *stands up.*

> **WC MORTEN**
> Madam.

> **CHRISTINE**
> Guilty!

> **WC MORTEN**
> Fifty years on Devil's Island.

> **CHRISTINE**
> Come on.

She strides off down the corridor, the others follow.

> **CHRISTINE**
> Guilty!

TIMMS *is standing with* BEVIN; *he has achieved only a very minor victory, most policemen would interpret it as a defeat.*

> **CHRISTINE**
> (referring to Timms)
> Know his problem? I can read him. No trouble. Can't get it up.

CHRISTINE *turns on her heel and is on her way out of the building, leaving* TIMMS, *stung, with unfinished business.*

---

33   EXT.   PUBLIC SCHOOL   DAY

SYDNEY's *Bentley moves at a gentle pace along a gravel driveway which leads to a minor English public school somewhere near Stevenage. Standing at the top of the stone steps leading to the front door, in school uniform, cap in hand, is* DAVID, CHRISTINE's *son.*

In the Bentley: SYDNEY *at the wheel,* CHRISTINE *sits next to him;* SHIRLEY *and* DOLLY *are in the rear seats.*

They are all dressed for CHRISTINE's *sister's wedding.*

SYDNEY *is dressed in a morning suit, his bald head buffed to a magnificent gloss.* CHRISTINE *is wearing a tight-fitting, royal blue, two-piece suit, blouse, and a small blue hat with a veil.*

SHIRLEY *wears a bright red dress, a coat and a large hat; and* DOLLY *is wearing a loose-fitting flower patterned dress and light top-coat. All are wearing carnation button-holes.*

SHIRLEY *and* DOLLY *are feeling high.* CHRISTINE *is excited, but agitated.*

> CHRISTINE
> (to Sydney, pointing to the steps)
> Over there, pull up over there, Sydney.

> SYDNEY
> What?

> CHRISTINE
> What?! Next you'll be saying balls to the general.
> (hits him)
> Over there!

SYDNEY *edges the Bentley to within a foot of the steps.*

> CHRISTINE
> (as she gets out)
> God knows why I'm sitting in the front.

> SHIRLEY
> Royalty in the back seat, dear.

> CHRISTINE
> Come on David — in!

DAVID *walks down the steps to the car.* DAVID *hates wearing his school uniform.*

> DAVID
> Why do I have to wear the uniform, mum?

> CHRISTINE
> (grabs cap, shoves it on his head)
> You wear your uniform. You put your cap on. In!

DAVID *is hustled into the back seat of the car.* SHIRLEY *and* DOLLY *cuddle sexily up to* DAVID, SHIRLEY *removes his cap.* CHRISTINE *gets into the front seat.*

> CHRISTINE
> Come on, Sydney.

Doors slam. The Bentley moves off down the drive, away from the school.
CHRISTINE *leans over the back, tries to put* DAVID's *cap back on his head.*

34   EXT.   CHURCH   DAY

A modern church in Harlow New Town.

A CROWD OF PEOPLE *stand outside the church,* GUESTS *and* BYSTANDERS, *waiting for the arrival of the bride. Excitement as somebody points. A large car heads towards the church – it's the Bentley.*

Inside the car:

> CHRISTINE
> Pull up!

> SYDNEY
> Where?

> CHRISTINE
> There! In front of the church for God's sake.

> SYDNEY
> I can't stop there.

> CHRISTINE
> You can.
> (hits him)
> Pull up!

> SYDNEY
> You need a chauffeur, that's what you need.

> CHRISTINE
> You keep quiet –

> SYDNEY
> And a butler.

> CHRISTINE
> – you and your little willy. Just keep quiet.

> SYDNEY
> What?

> CHRISTINE
> Balls to the general. Shut up.

> SYDNEY
> I haven't got a little willy.

> CHRISTINE
> Yes, you have. It's your most striking feature.

SYDNEY
Fine conversation to be having in front of your son.

SYDNEY *gets out from behind the steering wheel, walks round the car to open the passenger door for* CHRISTINE *who emerges, all smiles, with a gentle, almost royal wave to the* PEOPLE *standing at the door of the church.*

CHRISTINE
Hello!
(to the others)
Come on, get a bloody move on.
(puts cap on David)
Cap!

'Oohs', 'Ahs' and a round of applause from the CROWD *as the Rolls-Royce with white ribbons pulls up behind the Bentley. The* BRIDE *has arrived but her grand entrance has been blocked by* CHRISTINE *and the Bentley.*

The CHAUFFEUR *in the Rolls toots the hooter, prompting* SYDNEY *to drive away in the Bentley.* CHRISTINE *runs back to the Rolls and taps on the back window.*

CHRISTINE
(very pleased to see them)
We're here. Hello! Hello, Dad, hello, Elizabeth. We're here.

In the back of the Rolls is ELIZABETH, CHRISTINE's *sister and* EDWARD, *her father.*

EDWARD
(winding down the window)
I thought it must be you.

ELIZABETH
(waves)
Hello.

CHRISTINE
Oh, you look lovely, Lizzie, you really do. I wish it was me. Mum should be here, shouldn't she? I wish Mum was here to see you now.

The Rolls begins to edge forwards to the church entrance where the BRIDESMAIDS *and the* PAGEBOY *are waiting to escort the* BRIDE *into the church.*

CHRISTINE
(as the car moves)
I'm going to watch you get out.

Apart from BYSTANDERS, CHRISTINE *and* CO., *all the other* GUESTS *have now gone into church.* SHIRLEY *and* DOLLY *feel slightly awkward.*

> CHRISTINE
> (to Shirley and Dolly)
> She looks lovely, she really does. It's the veil that does it.
> Look at my Dad. That's my Dad.

CHRISTINE *takes out her Instamatic.*

ELIZABETH, *in full bridal gown with a long, flowing train, gets out of the Rolls-Royce, helped by* EDWARD, *her father, who is wearing a morning suit with top hat, gloves, etc.*

CHRISTINE *takes her snap.*

> CHRISTINE
> Gotcha! Hello, Aunt Winnie!

AUNT WINNIE *adjusts the* BRIDE's *train and puts the* BRIDESMAIDS *and* PAGEBOY *in place.* EDWARD *notices* DAVID *but does not acknowledge him.* DAVID *is more than aware of this.*

CHRISTINE
(to her father)
Give us a kiss. Go on. Cheer up.

She kisses him on the cheek.

EDWARD
Don't cover me in lipstick. Why don't you go into church?

CHRISTINE
I wish Mum could see this, you look so smart.

EDWARD
Don't go on, she's been dead nineteen years.

CHRISTINE
It's still a pity she's missed it. Say hello to your
grandfather, David.

EDWARD
(moves away)
This is your sister's day.

CHRISTINE
I wish it was me.

AUNT WINNIE
Ready!

EDWARD
I don't want it spoilt for her.

CHRISTINE
(kisses him again)
Don't worry, Dad, three pairs of knickers and that smile —
nothing'll get through to Lizzie.
(to Elizabeth, crosses her fingers)
Good luck!
(to the others)
Come on!

35   INT.   THE CHURCH   DAY

A very large turn-out for the wedding. Everybody, with the exception of
CHRISTINE *and CO., is in place for the wedding ceremony waiting for the*
arrival of the bride.

Organ music playing gently in the background.

They make a 'quiet' entrance into the church. DAVID *takes off his cap.*
CHRISTINE *grabs it and puts it back on his head.*

CHRISTINE
Put it on.

DAVID
We're in church.

CHRISTINE
Take it off, then. Take it off.

CHRISTINE *knocks the hat off* DAVID's *head.*

Standing at the end of the aisle is a POLICE SUPERINTENDENT *in full uniform.*

SHIRLEY
It's the old bill.

CHRISTINE
That's Edgar. My sister's marrying a copper, silly cow.

SHIRLEY
Takes all sorts.

All heads turn as CHRISTINE *leads them down the aisle, high-heels clacking on the stone floor. As* CHRISTINE *works her way towards the front of the church, she picks out friends and relations.*

CHRISTINE
Hello ... hello ...

The BRIDE *and her* ESCORTS *begin to move up the aisle. As this carefully rehearsed procession moves slowly on its course,* SYDNEY *appears at the back of the church. He has not the slightest notion where to find* CHRISTINE. *His bald head bobs and weaves behind the procession as he searches row after row for* CHRISTINE & CO.

As the BRIDE *reaches the* GROOM, SYDNEY *reaches* CHRISTINE.

CHRISTINE
(whispers)
Here ... in here. What are you doing here?

SYDNEY
What do you mean?

CHRISTINE
Aren't you Jewish?

SYDNEY
(taken aback)
What?

CHRISTINE
Because, if you are, you're not supposed to be in here. It's a church.

SYDNEY
(wrongly accused)
I know it's a church. And I'm not Jewish.

EDWARD *joins them in the front pew, frowns at them for making a noise.*

She makes SYDNEY *sit on the farthest side from her* FATHER.

The organ music stops. The VICAR *begins.*

> **VICAR**
> Before we begin, a word about photographs. As a mark of respect to Edgar and Elizabeth I would ask the congregation to refrain from taking photographs until the signing of the register ... We have come together ...

The VICAR *begins the service.* CAMERA *moves in on* CHRISTINE. *She bites her lip, hanky at the ready.*

AND INTO:

36   EXT.   CHURCH   DAY
_____

Electric church bells. CHRISTINE *follows the* BRIDE *and* GROOM *out of the church to discover* THIRTY YOUNG POLICEMEN *(cadets) blocking the entrance.*

> **CHRISTINE**
> Jesus Christ — we're surrounded!

The CADETS *raise their truncheons — to form the triumphal guard of honour. The confetti flies.*

> **CHURCH WARDEN**
> No confetti! Please, no confetti!

CHRISTINE *dives into the fray and emerges from the crush covered with confetti. Joining the trail of other* GUESTS, *she walks with* SHIRLEY *towards the reception hall.*

> **CHRISTINE**
> I kneed one of those coppers in the goolies.

> **SHIRLEY**
> Which one?

> **CHRISTINE**
> The tall one. I quite fancy him.

> **SHIRLEY**
> What animal has a shit on the end of a piece of string?

> **CHRISTINE**
> What?

> **SHIRLEY**
> A police dog.

They both crack up into helpless laughter.

---

37   INT.   RECEPTION HALL   DAY

A local hall used for receptions, amateur dramatics, and other functions.

Inside the hall, a champagne buffet reception is in progress. A happy occasion. GUESTS *are either standing or sitting at tables arranged round the perimeter of the hall. A real crush of people, shoulder to shoulder.*

On a table at the end of the hall is a four-tier wedding cake. The buffet is arranged on tables at either side. The BRIDE *and* GROOM *stand together, near the wedding cake. Everybody wants to speak to them to offer their congratulations.*

DOLLY *shakes hands with* ELIZABETH, *then* EDGAR. *Smiles all round.* EDGAR *kisses* CHRISTINE *on the cheek.* CHRISTINE *kisses* ELIZABETH.

        DOLLY
        (to Elizabeth)
        Congratulations. I like your dress.

ELIZABETH
Thank you.

CHRISTINE
Straight out of *Woman's Realm*. And Edgar . . .
(taps Edgar)
Edgar. This is Dolores.

EDGAR
How do you do?

DOLLY
Congratulations. I hope you'll be very happy.

ELIZABETH
Thank you, Dolores.

EDGAR
Yes, thank you.
(to Christine)
You don't know my mother.

CHRISTINE
No, I don't.

EDGAR *indicates an elderly* LADY *standing beside him.* MRS EDWINA
CHARLOTTE WINTER.

EDGAR
This is my mother.

CHRISTINE
(surprised)
Oh! I didn't think she'd still be alive. This is Edgar's
mother, Dolly.

DOLLY
Hello, dear.

CHRISTINE
Come on, Dolly, let's find us both a husband.

CHRISTINE *and* DOLLY *move across the hall.* CHRISTINE *stops and
says 'hello' to various* RELATIONS, *lots of laughter and kisses, a friendly
bunch, they are obviously very fond of* CHRISTINE. *They top up on
champagne as they go. Half-way across the hall, they meet up with and collect*
SHIRLEY *who has been chatting with Christine's relations.*

The three women plough on through the CROWD. CHRISTINE *sees her*
FATHER.

CHRISTINE
(grabs her father)
Dad. Dad. This is Dolores and this is Shirley, my friends
and business associates.

Having downed a few champagnes, EDWARD PAINTER *is in an expansive mood. He is not without charm. He shakes hands with* DOLLY *and* SHIRLEY.

> EDWARD
> How do you do?

> DOLLY
> Hello.

> EDWARD
> (to Shirley)
> How do you do?

> SHIRLEY
> Oh, extremely well, thank you, Mr Painter.

> CHRISTINE
> Dad's a widower, so watch your step.

> DOLLY
> Oh, really?

> CHRISTINE
> He's never married — well, not since Mum died.

> EDWARD
> A confirmed bachelor.

> CHRISTINE
> Nineteen years.

> DOLLY
> What a waste.

> EDWARD
> Thank you.

He kisses DOLLY*'s hand.*

> EDWARD
> Your friend has excellent taste, Christine.

He laughs at his own joke and moves on.

> CHRISTINE
> (to Edward, as he goes)
> David's over there, somewhere.

> CHRISTINE
> I think he fancies you, Dolly.

> DOLLY
> Chance would be a fine thing. I'm about to fill my knickers.

CHRISTINE
Me too, I'm busting.

CHRISTINE *and* DOLLY *head for the exit.*

---

38   INT.   LADIES LAVATORY   DAY

CHRISTINE *and* DOLLY *on the loo. Groans of relief.*

CHRISTINE
Oh, God, that's better. A running buffet, more like a
stampede. She's a mean cow, my sister. Tuppence says
there's marge in the bridge rolls.
(realises there's no loo paper)
Oh Gawd.

CHRISTINE *opens the loo door. Tights and knickers round her ankles, gets
off the loo and, still in that crouched position, shuffles to the door.*

CHRISTINE
(muttering)
She's got it all organised. And Edgar. Have you ever seen
anything more boring than Edgar? What a fart, eh?
There's no loo roll in here, can —

CHRISTINE *looks round the door post into* DOLLY's *cubicle, giving the
door a shove, catching* DOLLY *in a standing position with her dress up,
knickers and tights down.*

CHRISTINE *screams.*

CHRISTINE
Ah!

Total shock. Revelation. Eureka!

CHRISTINE
Dolly! Aah! Dolly . . .
(points)
you've . . . you've got a willy, Dolly! Aah! A willy! You're a
man, Dolly.

DOLLY
No, I'm not and there's no paper in here either.

CHRISTINE
But you've got a willy.

DOLLY
I know I have.

CHRISTINE
Quick. Let me look. I want to see. Show me. I don't believe
it. Quick, let me have a look.

DOLLY *sighs*.

> **DOLLY**
> Oh ... all right. It's nothing to be proud of.

CHRISTINE *is still standing with her skirt up and, like* DOLLY, *her tights and knickers round her knees.*

DOLLY *raises her skirt to reveal his penis – just as* MRS EDWINA CHARLOTTE WINTER, *Edgar's mother, enters the lavatory.*

Paralysis descends. Nobody moves. Then:

> **CHRISTINE**
> (almost jubilant)
> Aah! Ah ha!

MRS WINTER *makes good her escape as* CHRISTINE's *scream turns into laughter. Total helpless laughter. Even* DOLLY *finds it difficult to control herself.*

CHRISTINE *covers her mouth with her hand. Laughter dies to silence.*

> DOLLY
> Oh, dear.

39   INT.   LANDING/LAVATORY EXIT   DAY

The lavatory door opens, a little at first, then the whole way.

With dress properly adjusted, CHRISTINE *peeps out. She creeps out of the lavatory followed by* DOLLY, *both still dangerously close to giggles.*

> DOLLY
> It's not a laughing matter.

CHRISTINE *tiptoes over to the top of the stairs. Looks down the staircase and listens. They begin the great descent, down into the entrance hall on the ground floor.*

CHRISTINE *and* DOLLY *reach the bottom of the stairs just as* EDWARD PAINTER *bursts out of the main reception hall to confront his daughter. There is an appalling sense of the inevitable in this situation for* EDWARD. *He is deeply wounded.*

> EDWARD
> How could you?

> CHRISTINE
> What?

> EDWARD
> (the ravages of despair)
> Don't play dumb with me, Christine, you know exactly
> what I mean.

> CHRISTINE
> What's the matter, Dad?

> EDWARD
> How could you do this to me?

> CHRISTINE
> What?

> EDWARD
> How could you bring a sexual pervert to your sister's
> wedding?

> CHRISTINE
> Who?

> EDWARD
> (suddenly angry)
> Who?! Who d'you think?

CHRISTINE
Dolly's not a pervert, are you, Dolly?

DOLLY *is getting very nervous.*

EDWARD
Oh, so you think it's normal, do you, a man prancing round in a woman's skirt?

CHRISTINE
I didn't know she was a man.

DOLLY
I'm not a man.

EDWARD
Just leave, the pair of you.

ELIZABETH *has come out of the reception room, followed by* EDGAR *and the best man,* JOHN.

EDWARD
(to Elizabeth)
I can handle this, you go straight back in there, all of you —

CHRISTINE
Poor little Lizzy.

ELIZABETH
(very upset)
I knew you were going to cause trouble. I knew it. You're disgusting. I hope I never see you again.

EDWARD
Edgar.

CHRISTINE
Oh, thank you very much, Elizabeth.

ELIZABETH
You've spoilt everything.

EDGAR
Elizabeth, don't upset yourself.

ELIZABETH
Ever since I was born.

CHRISTINE
(to Dolly)
Can you hear this?

ELIZABETH
I hate you.

CHRISTINE
It's us that needs protecting –

EDGAR
(to Elizabeth)
Go back in.

CHRISTINE
– protecting from her mouth.

EDGAR
Now, that's enough.

CHRISTINE
Just stand clear when she opens her gob.

A sudden flash of temper from EDGAR.

EDGAR
(points a rigid finger at Christine)
Right! Now just one moment!

JOHN
Steady, Edgar.

EDGAR
I was against this from the start and now I know I was
right.

CHRISTINE
(to Dolly)
This is my brother-in-law.

DOLLY
Christine –

SHIRLEY *comes out of the reception hall, calm, detached and dangerous. She*
follows the action.

EDGAR
If I was on duty I would take a very serious view of this
matter.

CHRISTINE
But you are in uniform.

EDWARD
It's not worth it, Edgar. She's always been like this,
always.

EDWARD, *in despair, walks out of the hall, away from the main entrance,*
away from the reception.

In the reception hall, GUESTS *are crowding round the glass panel doors to*
catch a glimpse of the action.

EDGAR
(straight on)
Charges can be brought for this kind of thing.

DOLLY
(upset)
Oh dear.

DOLLY *heads back up the stairs.*

CHRISTINE
Dolly! Don't be a silly cow, stay here.

EDGAR
(to Dolly)
Where do you think you're going?

DOLLY
To the toilet.

EDGAR
Oh, no you're not!

DOLLY
I need a wee.

EDGAR
You stay out of the ladies lavatory — and the gents!

CHRISTINE
You piddle where you want, Dolly.

DOLLY
Is there a handicap toilet? Can I use that?

EDGAR
You stay out of *all* the toilets!

CHRISTINE
Stupid fart!

SHIRLEY *steps in, calm, but dangerous.*

SHIRLEY
(to Edgar, now outnumbered)
This is a very silly conversation and you are a very
naughty boy — and you know what happens to naughty
boys, don't you? Come along, Dolly. You too, Christine.

SHIRLEY *takes* DOLLY's *arm and leads her out of the building.*
CHRISTINE *pokes her head round the reception hall door.*

CHRISTINE
(cutting through the racket)
David!

CHRISTINE, DOLLY *and* SHIRLEY *repair to the Bentley, followed by* SYDNEY *and* DAVID.

> SYDNEY
> What's the hurry, doll? I was just beginning to enjoy myself. What's going on?

A gang of POLICE CADETS *are hanging around, looking rather sheepish.* SYDNEY *unlocks the car,* CHRISTINE *and CO. get in.*

> POLICE CADET
> Excuse me, is this your car?

> CHRISTINE
> It's not bloody stolen, if that's what you mean. Cheeky bugger.

The Bentley drives off – tin cans and toilet rolls (stolen from the ladies lav) are tied to the back of the car. They make an appalling racket. The POLICE CADETS *look at each other and shrug.*

No more than a few yards along the road, the Bentley jerks to a halt and SYDNEY, *furious, gets out of the car and begins yanking at the tin cans and toilet rolls.*

CHRISTINE *sees* EDWARD, *he has escaped into a recreation ground on the other side of the road.* CHRISTINE *looks at her father and then walks towards the entrance.*

The recreation ground is a drab locale, surrounded by council houses.

EDWARD, *head down, walks aimlessly out on to the open expanse of grass.* CHRISTINE, *her heels sinking into the ground, does her best to follow him.*

> CHRISTINE
> Dad! . . . Dad!

He does his best to ignore her.

> CHRISTINE
> Come here, Dad.

He stops, refuses to look at her, hopes she'll go away.

> CHRISTINE
> I'm sorry, Dad, I really am. When I came here I was happy, I really was.

She tries to touch him, make physical contact, to give him comfort. She's close to tears.

> CHRISTINE
> Come on, don't be like this, Dad, don't upset yourself. It's your day today too, you know, I'd do anything to make you happy. I'm so sorry.

Some success, he allows her to take his arm.

CHRISTINE
Come on. I'm sorry, Dad, I really am. Kiss me a kiss and say you love me.

She's almost made it.

EDWARD
You've spoilt it for her, how could you do it?

CHRISTINE
She spoilt it for herself.

EDWARD
What do you mean?

CHRISTINE
Look what she married.

EDWARD
(breaks away)
There you go again.

CHRISTINE
Dad, come on, he's a right box of farts and well you know it.

EDWARD
You can't say that.

CHRISTINE
I just have.

EDWARD
It's a respectable marriage, he is a police superintendent and a freemason —

CHRISTINE
He's a bum-hole, Dad, a fart in a box.

EDWARD
And he doesn't hang around with sexual perverts.

CHRISTINE
How do you know?

EDWARD
Listen to your mouth. You should be ashamed.

CHRISTINE
Well, I'm not.

EDWARD
And that's what's wrong with you.

CHRISTINE
(exasperated)
Dad, I'm not a bloody baby any more — that's what's wrong with Lizzie — I'm a woman. I've had babies and abortions —

EDWARD
Abortions?

CHRISTINE
Yes!

EDWARD
Why didn't you tell me? Abortions? Why didn't you tell me?

CHRISTINE
It's none of your bloody business! I told you when I was up the duff and you spat in my face.

EDWARD
That was different.

CHRISTINE
How many bastards can one girl take?

EDWARD
How can you talk like that? He's your son.

CHRISTINE
You're telling me that, you've noticed, have you? You do surprise me.

EDWARD
What's that supposed to mean?

CHRISTINE
You know what I mean. You've not so much as looked at him, not since we got here —

EDWARD
(begins to shake his head)
No . . .

EDWARD *totally rejects this line of accusation.*

CHRISTINE
You've not so much as looked at him for fourteen years!

EDWARD
(shaking his head)
No . . .

CHRISTINE
You've not looked at him, spoke to him, not a 'hello' not so much as a whisper. You make me feel like nothing.

> **EDWARD**
> (getting back)
> What do you think I've been doing all day?
>
> **CHRISTINE**
> He's your grandson!
>
> **EDWARD**
> It's your sister's wedding!
>
> **CHRISTINE**
> He's your only grandson! How many pups do you think
> that pair are going to spawn?
>
> **EDWARD**
> At least their children will have a father.

CHRISTINE *gives up for a moment, closes her eyes, holding in the tears.*

> **CHRISTINE**
> God, you're a liar, Dad, listen to you, you're such a bloody
> liar. Mum would never have treated me like this.

Rather than show her tears, she turns and walks away from her father, back across the soft turf of the recreation ground.

> **EDWARD**
> The news would have killed her ... if she hadn't been dead
> already. She'd have slammed the door in your face.

CHRISTINE *stops, provoked, bitterly wounded. She turns and advances on her father.*

> **CHRISTINE**
> I'm a prostitute. There. Spread that round the freemasons.
> Your daughter is a tart, on the game. Spread that round
> the next lodge meeting, I'd be glad of the custom.

EDWARD *turns a deathly pale, bones turned to clay.*

> **CHRISTINE**
> Shirley, my best friend, Shirley, she's a tart and so am I.
> And Dolly, our best friend Dolly, is a prostitute's maid.
> Always somebody else's daughter, eh?
> (tears coming up)
> Don't call my boy a bastard again. He's my son and I love
> him.

She turns and walks away, heels sinking into the ground, away from her father, a shattered man.

CHRISTINE *turns, tears streaming down her face –*

> **CHRISTINE**
> You silly bugger.

– and walks on again.

MIX to:

41   EXT.   SPAIN   NIGHT

A small courtyard surrounded by old buildings. Mimosa, bougainvillaea, and other flowers and trailing plants spill out from crumbling terracotta pots, climb up the wall and trail along balconies. The sea is close by. The sound of cicadas.

A room with a balcony lit by moonlight. It is warm and humid. Lying in a bed, naked, and covered only by a sheet, is CHRISTINE. *She is restless, unable to sleep.*

Unable to lie down any longer, she sits up on the edge of the bed, her feet on the floor. Her body is suntanned. She looks beautiful. She sighs, runs her hand down her thighs.

She puts on a cotton kaftan and walks out on to the balcony, out to where the air is cooler. It is late, everything is quiet. She stands for some moments, relaxed and alone, until she gradually becomes aware that she is being watched.

On the opposite side of the square, sitting out on a balcony, is THE MAN *– as seen by* CHRISTINE *outside the New Victoria café. He is sitting, smoking a cigarette, and drinking a glass of cool wine. And now he is watching* CHRISTINE. CHRISTINE *recognises him, knows him, but cannot quite place him.*

CHRISTINE *suddenly feels very vulnerable, disarmed, self-conscious at having been caught with her defences down.*

She stares back at THE MAN, *but is unable to speak. There is a tenderness in the way* THE MAN *looks at* CHRISTINE, *it is obvious that he finds her attractive.*

THE MAN *takes a final draw on his cigarette and puts it out. With half a smile, warm and gentle, he stands and walks back into the apartment. It is as he stands that* CHRISTINE *sees that he is naked – a fact which* THE MAN *makes no attempts to conceal.*

CHRISTINE *does not move, she continues to look across at the balcony. She trembles slightly, silently thrilled by this sudden encounter.*

A decision moves her. She walks back into the bedroom, hesitates, then selects a pair of briefs from her suitcase and puts them on. She looks back across the square to the balcony.

Lit only by moonlight, she looks at herself in the mirror. She brushes her hair and again looks at herself in the mirror. Her breasts are quite visible through the cotton kaftan. She is still trembling slightly.

She looks back across the square once more, then heads for the door.

42   EXT.   THE SQUARE   NIGHT

CHRISTINE *walks into the deserted courtyard, barefoot, wearing only her kaftan and briefs.*

She looks up to THE MAN's *balcony. She walks silently in the moonlight across the stone courtyard towards a door on the opposite side.*

At the door, she carefully turns the iron handle. Everything is quiet, the click of the door handle echoes up the stone marble stairs beyond. The door swings silently open.

Heart pounding, CHRISTINE *walks in through the doorway.*

43   INT.   MARBLE STAIRCASE   NIGHT

CHRISTINE *walks up the marble staircase to what she calculates to be the correct floor, stops, checks her bearings.*

She walks silently to the door. A surge of excitement – the door is slightly open. She waits, trembling, then puts out her hand and gently pushes the door, which swings open, letting her into THE MAN's *apartment.*

The apartment is in darkness.

CHRISTINE *stands in the entrance hall. She tiptoes towards what she calculates to be* THE MAN's *bedroom.*

Again, the door is slightly open.

She stops. Listens. From within the apartment, she can hear a noise – faint, indistinct. She ventures on until she can get a clear view into the bedroom.

The sound becomes more distinct – the warm sound of bodies touching, the tempered breath of two people making love.

On the bed: THE MAN *and a* WOMAN *making love. A vision of pure sensuality and erotic love, each locked within the other's potency and sexual power – totally unaware of* CHRISTINE.

CAMERA *concentrates on* CHRISTINE *standing in the hall, beyond the door, transfixed, like a child, unable to avert her eyes from what she sees.*

CUT TO:

44   EXT.   TELEPHONE KIOSK   DAY
                    NEAR A BEACH IN SPAIN

On the outside looking in: CHRISTINE *is on the telephone, attempting to make a telephone call to England.*

She is wearing shorts and a blouse, sunglasses on the top of her head, looking a little sun-scorched.

> CHRISTINE
> Hello...? Hello... Dolly? Is that you, Dolly? Shirley? I
> can't hear you. Can you hear me?
> (makes contact)
> Ah! Hello! Yes...yes. It's hot. Yes. I've got a bit of a rash.
> There's bodies everywhere. Hello! Oh, pillocks. Poxy
> phone.

She slams down the phone, stamps out of the kiosk, remembers something, goes back into the kiosk and collects her straw hat.

---

45   INT.   THE PINK BEDROOM   DAY

The door to the bathroom-en-suite swings open. Standing in the doorway is the expansive frame of MR MARPLES, dressed as THE SCHOOLBOY. He wears the complete outfit, including shorts, cap, satchel and blazer, all specially tailored for this fully grown adult male.

A voice is heard.

> SHIRLEY
> Out!

THE SCHOOLBOY *looks cowed but does not move.*

> SHIRLEY
> Come out!

THE SCHOOLBOY *shuffles into the exotic, faded luxury of the Pink Bedroom. SHIRLEY is dressed in a calf-length black skirt, a white blouse, black stockings, high heels, and her hair tied back in a bun. The Governess.*

> SHIRLEY
> What have we here?

Before THE SCHOOLBOY can answer, a loud hammering cuts into the drama, spoiling SHIRLEY's performance. SHIRLEY goes to the door, puts her head out into the hall where a man, MAC, is doing some carpentry work. MAC wears glasses – quite distinctive glasses.

DOLLY *walks out of the kitchen with a cup of coffee on a tray.*

> SHIRLEY
> Can you keep it down a minute, Mac?

> MAC
> Sorry.

SHIRLEY *closes the door.*

> SHIRLEY
> That's better. Now, what have we here, Auntie Christine?

CHRISTINE *is sitting on the pink sofa, trying to look strict. Suntan evidence of her Spanish holiday. She is holding a large dunce's cap.*

THE SCHOOLBOY
(whispers)
A naughty boy.

SHIRLEY
What?! Speak up!

THE SCHOOLBOY
I've been a naughty boy, Nana.

SHIRLEY
Hah! Another naughty boy, eh? The world is full of
naughty schoolboys.
(snaps)
What's the naughty boy done?

THE SCHOOLBOY
I was late for school.

SHIRLEY
What? Did you hear that, Auntie Christine? Late for
school. This is very serious, Auntie Christine.

CHRISTINE *is trying not to laugh.*

CHRISTINE
I'm sorry, Nana.

SHIRLEY
I can't stand boys being late for school. You are a naughty
little bugger!

SCHOOLBOY
(mumbles)
I'm sorry, Nana.

SHIRLEY
What does Nana do to little boys who are late for school,
tell me, what does she do?

SCHOOLBOY
Gives them a smack, Nana.

SHIRLEY
Correct! Where? Where does she smack them?

SCHOOLBOY
On ... on their bot-bots.

SHIRLEY
(majestically)
On their bot-bots! Yes. Every naughty boy gets a smack on
his bot-bot. Over! Bend over!

SCHOOLBOY
Yes, Nana.

SHIRLEY
(looks at Christine)
Right over.

SCHOOLBOY
Yes, Nana.

As if from nowhere, SHIRLEY produces a tawse (a split leather strap) and dispenses a swashbuckling thwack to THE SCHOOLBOY's bot-bot. He trembles as the thrill passes through his fundament and on to other regions.

MR MARPLES
(under his breath)
Please don't leave any marks.

SHIRLEY
Say 'thank you' to Nana.

SCHOOLBOY
Thank you, Nana.

THE SCHOOLBOY *is still bending over. Tension as he waits for the* coup de grâce. SHIRLEY *walks slowly to the front end. A glance at* CHRISTINE *and* –

SHIRLEY
You disgusting little bugger!

– SHIRLEY *clouts* THE SCHOOLBOY *hard round each ear. Neat and firm, sharp whacks, first with one hand, then the other.*

THE SCHOOLBOY
Oh!

THE SCHOOLBOY *quivers as he creams his underpants. He slowly straightens up. His face looks clearer, released from tension.*

MR MARPLES
Thank you, Nana.

MR MARPLES *looks at his watch, snaps into a completely different persona.*

MR MARPLES
Good lord, look at the time. Can't be caught tiffling around like this.

He bustles out of the pink bedroom towards the bathroom.

---

46   INT.   THE NEW VICTORIA CAFE   DAY

Tea-time. The same day.
CHRISTINE, SHIRLEY *and* DOLLY *at their usual table. They are giving the once over to the* MALE CUSTOMERS *in the café.*

CHRISTINE
Him.

SHIRLEY
Sad and hopeless. Comes his cocoa before he's got the plonker on.

SHIRLEY *reads men like others read newspapers.* CHRISTINE *stares at the* MAN *in question.*

CHRSITINE
Don't look it. What about him?

SHIRLEY
Which one?

CHRISTINE
There.

SHIRLEY
Bent as a box of frogs, dear.

CHRISTINE
He looks nice.

SHIRLEY
Maybe he is, I don't know. Most men don't like sex that much, can't wait to get it over.

CHRISTINE
They're only after one thing, if they didn't want it, we'd be out of a job.

SHIRLEY
I didn't say want, Christine, I said like. I said they didn't like it.

CHRISTINE
What about your Ron?

SHIRLEY
Enjoys a good cuddle, just like me.

A tap on the window. CHRISTINE *looks up. Standing just the other side of the glass, smiling, holding the theodolite, is* THE MAN. *He smiles, mouths 'Hello'.*

CHRISTINE
(blushes)
Oh, my God.

MAN *signals 'Come outside'.*

CHRISTINE
Let me out, let me out!

> DOLLY
> Wasp up her bum.

JACKIE *arrives with fresh cups of tea as* CHRISTINE *makes a dash for the door.*

> SHIRLEY
> (searching her shopping bag)
> Oh, bumoles, I've left my butter in the fridge at the flat.

> JACKIE
> I'll nick you some.

> SHIRLEY
> Ta.

CHRISTINE *has run out of the café where she meets* THE MAN. *They shake hands, all smiles, as* WC MORTEN *arrives at the café carrying camera equipment. He walks into the café.*

> WC MORTEN
> Madam has a fancy man.

> SHIRLEY
> Sit down and shut up.

> WC MORTEN
> Yes, lady.

Outside, THE MAN *writes something on a card and gives it to Christine. They shake hands.* CHRISTINE *walks back into the café and sits down.*

> DOLLY
> What are you having tonight?

> SHIRLEY
> Fillet steak, mange-tout, bottle of beaujolais.

> CHRISTINE
> I've got a date.

> WC MORTEN
> Yes, Madam.

> CHRISTINE
> (like a child, trembling)
> I've got a date.

47   INT.   CHRISTINE'S FLAT   NIGHT

CHRISTINE *is standing on the table.* WC MORTEN *is lying on his back on the floor holding a camera.*

> WC MORTEN
> No, no, Madam's just not trying.

> **CHRISTINE**
> This dirty bugger's looking up my skirt.

> **WC MORTEN**
> Nice angle.

> **CHRISTINE**
> Yes, up my skirt.
> (to Shirley)
> These boots are too tight.

CHRISTINE *is wearing a pair of brown knee-high leather boots, a black plastic mac, black bra, black suspenders and black stockings.*

WC MORTEN *gets up off the floor, goes over to his shoulder pack and delves within. He has rigged up some lights, the purpose being to take photographs of* CHRISTINE. RON, SHIRLEY*'s husband, is fiddling with wires and a plug.* SHIRLEY *is in charge of wardrobe and* DOLLY *is looking through a contacts magazine called* Adult Contacts.

> **DOLLY**
> Are we putting ads in all these magazines?

> **WC MORTEN**
> We must appeal to a broad spectrum of the deviant population.

> **DOLLY**
> Suffer the little perverts . . .

> **CHRISTINE**
> Oh, God, I feel sick up here.

> **WC MORTEN**
> Here, Madam, this is what we're after.

WC MORTEN *holds up and shows* CHRISTINE *some photographs from a fem-dom magazine (he has quite a collection). He flicks through the pages.*

> **CHRISTINE**
> (reads)
> 'Get him under, keep him under' — she's sitting on his face!
> Disgusting! I'm not going to pose for no porno magazine.

> **SHIRLEY**
> Christine, you're not posing for a pornographic magazine.

> **WC MORTEN**
> No, no, Nadam — not for that, here —
> (takes Dolly's contact mag)
> — this is a sexual contacts directory. Very respectable.

> **SHIRLEY**
> Try to look kinky, you look like you're waiting for a bus.

SHIRLEY *does up the belt on the plastic mac, tries to make* CHRISTINE *look more fem-dom.*

CHRISTINE
(still on the table)
What if my husband saw it?

SHIRLEY
You're not married.

CHRISTINE
I might be. Not going to spend the rest of my days sitting on somebody's face.

DOLLY
(reads)
'The dungeon of delight. If you can take it, I can give it.'

CHRISTINE
Sounds horrible.

DOLLY
(reads)
'Beginners welcome.'

RON
(still fiddling with the plug)
Is it brown at the top?

WC MORTEN *is on the floor again, squinting through the camera.*

WC MORTEN
Michelle, in Earls Court, used to do group bookings in her mediaeval torture chamber. She gave me a discount.

CHRISTINE
Why did she give you a discount?

WC MORTEN
I did the mopping up, Madam, I cleared up the other fellows' cocoa.

CHRISTINE
Disgusting! Do you know how to use that thing?

WC MORTEN
Aerial photographer, Madam, World War Two. I once photographed Hitler on the lavatory. Come along, let it rip!

SHIRLEY
(gives Christine a whip)
Here, use this. Look sadistic.

CHRISTINE
Sadistic?

> **WC MORTEN**
> Look superior, Madam.
>
> **SHIRLEY**
> Just look horrible. Stick out your crutch. Be sadistic.
>
> **WC MORTEN**
> Yes, please.
>
> **RON**
> (has finished the plug)
> Right.
>
> **CHRISTINE**
> I don't mind being sadistic —
>
> **RON**
> Now then.
>
> **CHRISTINE**
> — as long as I don't have to hurt anyone.

RON *pushes the plug into the socket and turns it on.*

> **RON**
> Here we go.

Bang! The plug explodes and all the lights go out.

Black out.

Pause.

> **RON**
> Oh, dear.

CUT TO:

---

48   INT.   THE PUNISHMENT ROOM   DAY

Morning.

The punishment room at the apartment with the pink bedroom. The punishment room is a completely bare room with bare white walls and shiny black linoleum on the floor.

A client, MR WEBB, a man in his late fifties, balding head, silver grey hair, stands in the corner. A quiet dignity about this person. He has a gold (brass) chain around his neck which is attached to a ring on the wall. He is wearing a woman's bikini.

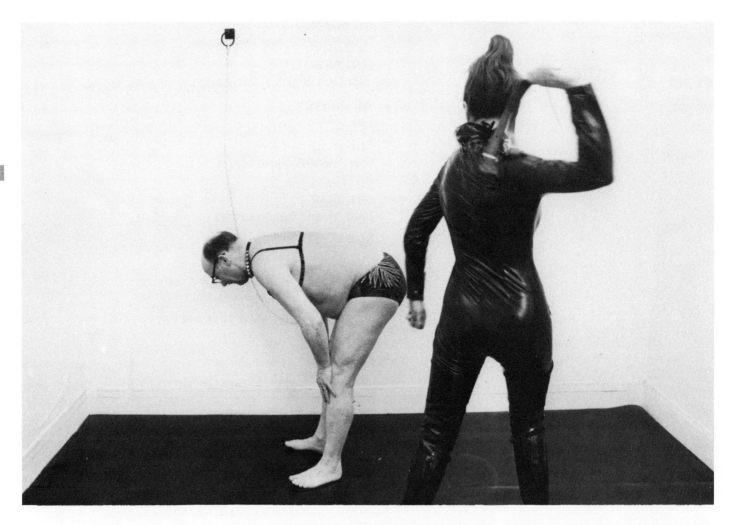

CHRISTINE, *wearing a black catsuit, strides into the room and over to* MR
WEBB.

        CHRISTINE
        Bend over.

MR WEBB *bends over.* CHRISTINE *smacks him hard on the arse with a
leather tawse.*

        CHRISTINE
        That's for the Inland bloody Revenue!

She marches out of the room. MR WEBB *straightens up, looking somewhat
worried.*

Out in the entrance hall:

CHRISTINE *walks out into the hall as* DOLLY *walks out of the bedroom
carrying a pair of rubber wellingtons.*

MAC *is still busy building the cupboard.*

> CHRISTINE
> Cheeky sods.

The front doorbell rings. DOLLY *opens the door to let in* WC MORTEN, *who is carrying a canvas bag.*

> DOLLY
> (to Christine)
> What's the matter with you today?

> WC MORTEN
> Good morning, ladies.

No response.

> CHRISTINE
> (to Dolly)
> Look what I got in the post this morning.

She produces a brown envelope with a window at the front. WC MORTEN *upturns the canvas bag and empties the contents – several dozen letters – on to the floor.*

> WC MORTEN
> The flood gates are open!

> DOLLY
> (ignores him, to Christine)
> What is it?

> CHRISTINE
> Inland bloody Revenue. From when I got nicked.

> WC MORTEN
> Box number 192. A plethora of kinky correspondence.

No response.

> CHRISTINE
> Cheeky sods assessed my earnings and sent me a bill for tax!

SHIRLEY *comes out of the Pink Bedroom. She is dressed as a nurse and wearing rubber gloves and a face-mask.*

> WC MORTEN
> Good morning, Mac.

No response.

> DOLLY
> (to Morten)
> You can't leave those there, you know.

> SHIRLEY
> (pulls down the mask)
> Some of us are working in here. Who's attending to Mr
> Webb's bot-bot?

CHRISTINE *shoves the tax demand back into her handbag and, tawse in hand, strides into the punishment room* –

> CHRISTINE
> Over!

– *smacks* MR WEBB *on the arse and out of the room in one continuous movement.*

And CUT TO:

49   INT.   THE PINK BEDROOM/THE APARTMENT   DAY

CAMERA IN CLOSE on three sets of knees in gymslips.

> SHIRLEY
> Oh, you're sitting here, are you? It's that new girl,
> Christine.

> CHRISTINE
> So it is.

CAMERA moves slowly out to reveal SHIRLEY *and* CHRISTINE *sitting on either side of* LIONEL *(mid thirties), a handsome man. He has muscular, hairy legs. All three people are dressed as schoolgirls in gymslips.*

> SHIRLEY
> Oh, this is nice. All schoolgirls together. No boys, just
> girls, all together.

LIONEL *is already quite excited by this scenario.*

> SHIRLEY
> (breaks off)
> Incidentally, Christine, if you ever need legal advice,
> Lionel is an excellent barrister, aren't you Lionel?

> LIONEL
> Oh, yes.

> SHIRLEY
> (back into fantasy, no break)
> Have you seen these dirty books those teachers have left
> lying around?

SHIRLEY *picks up a sex magazine and flicks through a few pages.*

> SHIRLEY
> 'Sex on Lesbos'. Oh, it makes me come over all lesbian.

       CHRISTINE
       Me too.

LIONEL *is enjoying the magazine.*

       SHIRLEY
       (looking at the mag)
       She's got nice legs.
       (to Lionel)
       So have you.
       (referring to Lionel)
       Hasn't she got nice legs?

       CHRISTINE
       Lovely.

       SHIRLEY
       I think she must be a lesbian — just like us. You're a
       lesbian, aren't you?

       LIONEL
       (dry in the mouth)
       Yes, I am.

CHRISTINE
Me too.

SHIRLEY
What lovely legs she's got. I love being a lesbian, don't you?

LIONEL
Yes, I do.

CHRISTINE
Me too.

SHIRLEY *leans over, looks at* CHRISTINE.

SHIRLEY
Polly parrot.

CHRISTINE
(nods towards Lionel)
Popozogolou?

SHIRLEY
(nods)
Popozogolou.

50   INT.   THE PUNISHMENT ROOM   DAY

The door to the punishment room smashes open. CHRISTINE *and* SHIRLEY, *still wearing gymslips, stride into the room like the Gestapo. They are well into the mood of things.*

MR WEBB *is still chained to the wall and wearing the bikini.*

SHIRLEY
This one wants golden rain, Miss Kane.

CHRISTINE
Does she now, Miss Stern?

SHIRLEY
Will you oblige, Miss Kane?

CHRISTINE
Let me at him, Miss Stern.
(mouths)
What's golden rain?

MR WEBB
Excuse me . . .

CHRISTINE
Yes?! Speak up!

MR WEBB
Excuse me, superior mistress, but how did you know I
worked for the Inland Revenue?

CHRISTINE
You work for the Inland Revenue?

MR WEBB
Yes. If you have any problems, it would be an honour to
serve.

DOLLY
(at the door)
Psst!

DOLLY *nods to* CHRISTINE *and* SHIRLEY – *something urgent in the
hallway. At the doorway,* CHRISTINE *grabs* SHIRLEY.

CHRISTINE
What's golden rain?

SHIRLEY
Piddle.

CHRISTINE
What?

SHIRLEY
He wants you to piddle on him.

CHRISTINE
I can't do that.

SHIRLEY
You've agreed to it now.

DOLLY
Come on!

51   INT.   HALLWAY/THE APARTMENT   DAY

Still in their gymslips, CHRISTINE *and* SHIRLEY *walk out of the punishment room and look towards the front door to see* TIMMS. *He is with* GIBSON, *another detective. They are both slightly pissed.* TIMMS *holds up his hands in a gesture of peace.*

TIMMS
Detective constables Timms and Gibson, Flying Squad. No more vice, just villains.

DOLLY *has grabbed the Ewbank hand sweeper and is furiously sweeping the carpet.* MAC *goes on building the cupboard.*

The moment TIMMS *sees* CHRISTINE, *he fancies her, can't keep his eyes off her.* CHRISTINE *is more than aware of this and, despite herself, likes it.*

CHRISTINE
(points to Dolly)
She's the cleaner, nothing more, nothing less, all right Mr Smart Arse?

TIMMS
I'm not interested.

SHIRLEY
They've been shifted, Christine, they're not vice squad.

CHRISTINE
Cheeky sods.

SHIRLEY
(moves towards the bedroom)
Put the kettle on, Dolly.

TIMMS
Can I use your toilet? I'm busting.

GIBSON
Yeah, me too.

> CHRISTINE
> They've come to use the bloody toilet.

CHRISTINE *and* SHIRLEY *look at each other. Click.*

> SHIRLEY
> Have they?

> CHRISTINE
> This way.

They take TIMMS *and* GIBSON *into the punishment room.* DOLLY *slows down on the Ewbank.* MAC *stops sawing a piece of wood. They look towards the punishment room.*

CUT TO:

---

52   INT.   BEDROOM/CHRISTINE'S FLAT   NIGHT

DOLLY *with a glass of Guinness, sits on* CHRISTINE'*s bed. She is watching* CHRISTINE *who, wearing only her slip, is ransacking her wardrobe for dresses. She is nervous, in a state of excitement and anxiety as she contemplates her date on the following evening.*

She takes out yet another dress, holds it up to her body, chucks it down.

> CHRISTINE
> Send that lot to the jumble.

On the mantelpiece: a shrine of family photographs. Father, mother, sister and David, her son. Resting in the corner of the frame of one of the photographs is the card given to her by THE MAN. *On it is written '7.45 p.m., Friday 23rd.'*

CHRISTINE *picks up the card, looks at it.*

> CHRISTINE
> How does she do it?
> (looks at Dolly)
> Shirley. How can she do the two? What about Ron? What does he think?

> DOLLY
> That's their business.
> (sips her Guinness)

> CHRISTINE
> He's so good-looking, Dolly. And charming. He's got such a gentle look in his eye, you know what I mean?

> DOLLY
> Who – Ron?

> CHRISTINE
> No, silly cow . . . you know who I mean.

CHRISTINE *thinks about* THE MAN.

> CHRISTINE
> Fed up with silly buggers, Dolly, no more naughty
> schoolboys, I'm getting out.

> DOLLY
> How will you pay the bills?

> CHRISTINE
> But I'll be married . . . Oh!
> (she covers her mouth, laughs)

The doorbell rings.

> CHRISTINE
> Oh, bugger.

She puts on her dressing-gown, heads for the door.

> CHRISTINE
> I could always do a bit on the side.

The doorbell rings again.

> CHRISTINE
> Pound says it's Sydney. I'll marry him.

Down the hall to the front door. She opens it.

It is SYDNEY, *in full evening dress.*

> SYDNEY
> Hello, doll.

CHRISTINE's *gaze shifts from* SYDNEY *to* SYDNEY's COMPAN-
ION, *also in evening dress. Her name is* PAT, *a thin, not unattractive woman
of thirty-eight, but dressed in an attempt to look younger.*

> SYDNEY
> This is Pat, doll. My fiancée. We're engaged to be married.
> (to Pat)
> This is Christine, doll.

Standing there in her dressing-gown, CHRISTINE *is suddenly aware that she
looks a wreck.*

> PAT
> (holds out her hand)
> Hello.

CUT TO:

In the hallway, near the front door, the attention is on the cupboard which MAC *has been building.*

As the CAMERA *moves forwards, we see that inside the cupboard there is a chair – no ordinary chair – it looks remarkably like an electric chair with restraining straps at the back, the neck, and at the arms and legs. A fine piece of craftsmanship.*

SHIRLEY, DOLLY *and* CHRISTINE *are strapping* MAC *into the chair. He is covered from head to foot by a tight-fitting rubber suit, including rubber gloves. Only the circle of his face is visible. And he is still wearing his glasses.*

The work progresses in a concentrated silence.

> SHIRLEY
> That's not too tight, is it?

MAC *shakes his head.* THE WOMEN *extract no enjoyment from this activity.*

> CHRISTINE
> That one round his neck looks tight.

> MAC
> It's fine.

The doorbell rings. CHRISTINE *leaps.*

> CHRISTINE
> Aah!

They look at each other, uncertain, caught in the act, wondering who might be on the other side of the door.

> SHIRLEY
> (whispers)
> Shut the door.

They shut the cupboard door, with MAC *still strapped in the seat.*

> DOLLY
> (takes command)
> Who is it?

> VOICE
> It is I, Mercury, the wingéd messenger, your obedient
> servant bringeth the post.

> DOLLY
> It's the Wing Commander.

Relief all round.

> CHRISTINE
> Silly sod.

DOLLY *opens the front door,* SHIRLEY *opens the cupboard door. Enter* WC MORTEN – *much to* MAC's *disapproval.*

> **WC MORTEN**
> Box number 192 at your service.

He empties several dozen letters from a canvas bag on to the hall floor.

> **DOLLY**
> (instantly niggled)
> Don't do that!

> **WC MORTEN**
> (sees Mac)
> Ah! Voyager One ready for take off. Tadgers at one o'clock!
> Dive, dive, dive!

> **MAC**
> Do we have to have this?

> **CHRISTINE**
> Belt up or bugger off.

> **WC MORTEN**
> Yes, Madam, certainly, Madam. You should put me in
> there, Madam.

> **MAC**
> Please!

> **WC MORTEN**
> Would he like me to sit on his face, Madam?

> **CHRISTINE**
> Out!

> **WC MORTEN**
> My turn next.

CHRISTINE *shoves* WC MORTEN *out of the front door.*

> **CHRISTINE**
> Go on. Shove off.

> **WC MORTEN**
> (leaving)
> Yes, Madam, certainly, Madam.

> **CHRISTINE**
> He's a sod.

> **SHIRLEY**
> He only does it to annoy you.
> (adjusts a strap)
> There.

> **MAC**
> Now the mask.

SHIRLEY *removes* MAC's *glasses and places a rubber mask over his eyes, leaving only his mouth visible. A strap is then placed round his head.*

> **MAC**
> Now. I wish to be left in the chamber for exactly one and one half hour. If I need any assistance I will press the alarm, here, and the light will come on.

He presses a button built into the arm of the chair and a small red light flashes on the outside of the cupboard.

> **MAC**
> Is it working?

> **DOLLY**
> Yes.

> **SHIRLEY**
> (repeats)
> Yes.

> **CHRISTINE**
> Can you hear us?

> **MAC**
> Yes. One and one half hour. Shirley, the gag, please.

SHIRLEY *straps a gag, which includes a large rubber dummy which goes into the mouth, round* MAC's *face. He is totally covered in rubber. An alien, ready for execution.* CHRISTINE *watches the final stages, total incomprehension at the spectacle before her.*

> **SHIRLEY**
> (to Mac)
> All right, slave. Now we are closing the doors for ever. The High Priestess will attend without.

SHIRLEY *closes the cupboard doors, sealing off* MAC *within.*

> **SHIRLEY**
> That's it. Home. Supper. Feet up in front of the telly.

SHIRLEY *puts on her coat, ready to go home.* DOLLY *gets her own coat, her bag, and* SHIRLEY's *shopping bag from the kitchen.*

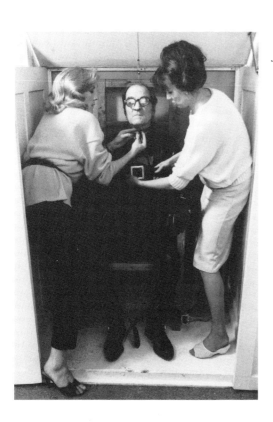

> **CHRISTINE**
> (keeping her voice down)
> He's such a nice man. I don't understand it, do you?

> **SHIRLEY**
> No, I don't.

> **CHRISTINE**
> I thought he was making a cupboard to hang our coats in. I did.

> (they laugh)
> It's a bit scarey, isn't it?

> DOLLY
> I'll stay if you want.

> SHIRLEY
> What time's your date?

> CHRISTINE
> I've got ages yet, you go.

DOLLY *kisses* CHRISTINE *on the cheek.*

> DOLLY
> Good luck.

> SHIRLEY
> He's just a feller. It's just a date.

> CHRISTINE
> I'm so nervous. I've got the colly-wobbles.

> SHIRLEY
> Go out. Enjoy yourself.

> CHRISTINE
> Ta.

SHIRLEY *kisses* CHRISTINE *on the cheek.* DOLLY *and* SHIRLEY *leave, closing the door behind them.*

> DOLLY and SHIRLEY
> (as the door closes)
> Bye.

CHRISTINE *is left alone in the hall, with* MAC *secure in the cupboard.*

She walks through into the RECEPTION ROOM: *it is early evening, a glimmer of warmth in the setting sun.*

She stares at a dress hanging in the room – a new dress, with new shoes, etc. A new outfit. Romantic. She stares at the dress for some time. Touches it. A sense of loneliness.

She sits on the sofa, opens her handbag, takes out the card. '7.45 p.m., Friday 23rd.' She looks at the card and places it on the mantelpiece beside a clock which says 6.01.

CUT TO:

54   INT.   THE HALLWAY/THE APARTMENT   DAY

A shot of the cupboard, the doors closed. MAC, *the rubberised alien fetishist, is trapped within.*

A sense of danger creeps into the proceedings. CUT TO:

55   INT./EXT.   RESTAURANT   NIGHT

A Spanish restaurant in Pimlico. Up-market, but casual. The perfect place for a romantic evening. So far, most of the tables are empty.

THE MAN arrives at the restaurant. It is obvious that he is known here. He talks to a WAITER, checks his watch, decides to take a drink at his reserved table in the window. CUT TO:

56   INT.   LIFT/THE APARTMENT MANSION BLOCK   NIGHT

The lift which serves the apartment.

HIGH SHOT: inside the lift shaft, precarious, looking down several floors to the lift cage on the ground floor.

The lift doors slam shut. The lift proceeds to the second floor. Stops. The lift doors crash open.

CAMERA, low, follows the footsteps of a MAN as he walks to the front door of the Pink Apartment.

A jangling of keys.

A key slides into the lock and turns . . .

CUT BACK TO:

57   INT.   RESTAURANT   NIGHT

THE MAN waits, sips his wine, and wonders if his date is going to show up.

58   INT.   RECEPTION ROOM/THE APARTMENT   NIGHT

Light from the window spills into the dark room. CAMERA moves slowly from CHRISTINE's dress, still hanging where we last saw it, on to the sofa.

Still sitting on the sofa is CHRISTINE. She is asleep. Like a rag doll, she has flopped slowly in her sleep to one side until her head met with a cushion.

CAMERA moves slowly in on her sleeping face until – from somewhere in the apartment – a noise jolts her violently into consciousness.

A moment of total confusion, of not knowing where she is. Then another noise brings her into focus. A powerful sense of danger, that all is not well. She checks her watch, it's 7.55 p.m.

She goes to the door, looks out into the darkened hallway. Another noise – another shock. The lights are on in the Pink Bedroom, shining into the hall, and the noise came from there. Without doubt, there is an intruder in the flat.

More than nervous, CHRISTINE moves quietly down the hallway, all of her focus on the bedroom door. As she creeps towards the bedroom door, she does not notice that the red light on the cupboard door is flashing.

CHRISTINE cautiously pokes her head round the bedroom door, scared witless of what she might see. The red light on the cupboard is flashing away behind her.

The room appears to be empty. Silence. She ventures a little further. Silence. Further still. Sudden shock. THE INTRUDER. She screams. So does THE INTRUDER. Both of them taken equally by surprise.

Standing by the full-length mirror, dressed in a pink bra, knickers, stockings and suspenders, red shoes and a transparent red tricot négligé (and black moustache) is MR POPOZOGOLOU. He falls backwards against the mirror and, in his red high heels, flaps like a trapped turkey.

> MR POPOZOGOLOU
> (at first incoherent, then –)
> Please ... No ... I'm sorry ... please ... sorry.

CHRISTINE has recognised him, but says nothing, just stares. MR POPOZOGOLOU stops flapping when he reaches the corner, knocking over the table lamp, and stares back.

> CHRISTINE
> ... Mr Popozogolou.

MR POPOZOGOLOU is distraught, near to tears. He picks up the lamp.

> MR POPOZOGOLOU
> If it is broken, I can fix it. I will pay for it. No problem. I fix it. OK? I fix it for you.

> CHRISTINE
> I thought some bloody lunatic had got into the flat. A robber. You can never tell these days, can you?

MR POPOZOGOLOU is in an extremely volatile condition. He fiddles with the lamp, switching it on and off.

> MR POPOZOGOLOU
> I think it's OK, yes, it's OK. It's working OK. Click, click. There. It's a good lamp.

CHRISTINE stays calm, tries to reassure him.

> CHRISTINE
> You look nice. You do, you really do. That outfit looks nice on you. It suits you. If I'd have known, if you'd told me, you could borrow my clothes any time you want. You can

come round here and dress up — I'll dress up with you, if you want — you don't have to come creeping in here, you know. You can wear whatever you want in here.

She has edged herself over to sit on the bed. She pats the space beside her, inviting MR POPOZOGOLOU *to sit down. He sits on the bed next to* CHRISTINE, *large tears begin to roll slowly down his face into his moustache.*

Behind them, in the hallway, the red light is still flashing in the cupboard.

> MR POPOZOGOLOU
> I am not a transvestite. I am not a homosexual.

> CHRISTINE
> I don't mind if you are.

> MR POPOZOGOLOU
> I love my wife.

> CHRISTINE
> That's nice.

MR POPOZOGOLOU *places* CHRISTINE's *hand against his breast.*

> MR POPOZOGOLOU
> I like to wear a dress.

The doorbell rings. They both jump.

> CHRISTINE
> Oh, my God!

> MR POPOZOGOLOU
> Red light. There. What is it?

> CHRISTINE
> (panic)
> Oh, no!

CHRISTINE *dashes to the cupboard in the hallway. The doorbell rings again. She goes to open the cupboard door but thinks better of it. She puts the safety chain on the front door and opens it, just a little. Standing at the door is* TIMMS: *slightly pissed, as usual, and in pursuit of his sexual obsession for* CHRISTINE.

> TIMMS
> Hello.

> CHRISTINE
> What do you want?

> TIMMS
> Friendly visit. Off duty. Peace. Pax. Come to check your locks.

> CHRISTINE
> I'm busy.

A beat. TIMMS smiles. He knows CHRISTINE fancies him.

> TIMMS
> Don't you ever get fed up?

> CHRISTINE
> What with?

> TIMMS
> All these kinky sods. Don't you ever ache for something
> straight?

> CHRISTINE
> Not that I've noticed.

> TIMMS
> I think you do. I know you do. It's written all over your
> face.

He's right. She hesitates.

> TIMMS
> Let me come in. Now.
> (smiles)
> Got to keep in with the police.

> CHRISTINE
> (suddenly turns sour)
> Sorry. Too late.

*She slams the door in TIMMS's face. Waits. MR POPOZOGOLOU
hovers near the bedroom door.*

*On the other side of the front door, TIMMS is left with the cold anger of
rejection. He walks off down the stairs.*

> CHRISTINE
> (panic rising)
> Oh my God, bloody hell!

*She pulls open the cupboard door – MAC, the Black Rubber Phantom, is still
strapped to the chair.*

> CHRISTINE
> (believing him to be dead)
> Mac! Are you alive or dead?

> MAC
> I'm alive.

59   INT./EXT.   RESTAURANT   NIGHT

Romantic MUSIC.

In the restaurant, COUPLES sit together at candle-lit tables.

THE MAN, still sitting in the window seat, gives up waiting for CHRISTINE. He pays for his drinks and leaves.

He walks out of the restaurant and crosses the road.

The wind blows cold along the street.

THE MAN stands at the kerb waiting for a taxi. He does not know that, standing a few feet behind him, in the shadows of a shop doorway, is CHRISTINE. Under her coat, she is wearing her new dress.

CHRISTINE watches him. He puts out his hand. A taxi slows down, stops. CHRISTINE is just feet away from him, standing in the shadows of the shop doorway.

THE MAN gets into the taxi. One word and CHRISTINE can still stop him. He is just one small step away.

The taxi drives off.

CHRISTINE walks out of the doorway to the spot where, seconds ago, THE MAN has been standing. She watches the taxi, almost out of view, lost in a stream of taxis.

Tears well up inside. The taxi has gone and she is left alone, staring into the void.

60   INT./EXT.   BEDROOM/HOUSE   DAY

A bedroom. No furniture, except a broken chair. Bare floorboards. An empty house.

Footsteps echo up the staircase. Voices. The door to the bedroom is opened. Enter WC MORTEN, CHRISTINE and MR GRIVAS, an estate agent.

WC MORTEN
This is very nice, Madam.

MR GRIVAS
There are three other bedrooms of this size, a smaller bedroom and a box-room.

WC MORTEN
That would be my room, Madam.

CHRISTINE
Put you in a bloody kennel.

WC MORTEN
Yes, please.

CHRISTINE *walks to the centre of the room. A chance to study* CHRISTINE *as she inspects the room. She has a different hair style, her make up is carefully tailored. She is wearing a fur coat and carries an expensive handbag. She is more mature, just as sharp and humorous, but less vulnerable.*

CHRISTINE
(after taking in the room)
Nice.

MR GRIVAS
They are well-proportioned rooms.

WC MORTEN
Very nice.

CHRISTINE
If you put up some of the cash, it gives you no rights over my life, you know.

WC MORTEN
(follows her out of the room)
Call it an indulgence, Madam, of an ageing pillock in the autumn of his days.

MR GRIVAS *takes the lead as* CHRISTINE *and* WC MORTEN *walk down the stairs. Bare floorboards down the staircase and in the hall.*

WC MORTEN
The perfect locale for a brothel, Madam. A house of pleasure. Privacy and discretion assured.

CHRISTINE
It's a home. My home. Not just a knocking shop.

WC MORTEN
The place for sex is in the home.

CHRISTINE *walks towards the conservatory at the end of the lounge and out into a large, overgrown garden beyond.*

WC MORTEN *follows* CHRISTINE *out into the garden.* MR GRIVAS *loiters in the background – mounting curiosity as to the nature of this unusual couple.*

WC MORTEN
A guaranteed loan, Madam. Through my bank. The bargain of a lifetime. Snap it up now before senile dementia runs me down.

CHRISTINE
This garden's a mess.

WC MORTEN
'Slaves required. Foot and shoe fetishists welcome. Household and gardening duties essential.' Won't cost a penny.

> CHRISTINE
> I'll leave that to you.

> WC MORTEN
> I'll take care of everything, Madam.

CHRISTINE *walks back towards the house.* MR GRIVAS, *gentleman, holds open the conservatory door.*

> CHRISTINE
> (to Grivas)
> Nice. A mess. A nice mess.

MIX TO:

---

61   EXT.   AN ALLEY   DAY

The quality of the film suddenly changes. We're into blown-up Super-8, badly scratched; this film has been projected a thousand times.

A YOUTH *drifts along the sidewalk. He's clean-cut, handsome, vulnerable beneath the cool macho exterior, and – most important of all – well stacked, loaded and ready to fire.*

Standing in the alley is a WOMAN *and she's looking in his direction. The slit in her skirt reaches up to her armpits. A tour guide of the essential hot spots and attractions: beneath the skin-tight pencil skirt, suspenders cling to the black silk stockings which lick their way down the thighs and beyond to five-inch stilettos. The blouse falls from the shoulder, fighting a losing battle with tender but firm flesh trapped within.*

TITLES OVER: 'Aldabra Films present SUCK AND SUCK AGAIN'

The lips part, glistening, savage red, as the WOMAN *draws deeply on a King Size Camel. Dark and dangerous, the eyes compel. There's no fighting the call.*

The YOUTH *makes his move. He walks – away from the sidewalk where honest, decent folk go about their business – drawn on by the heat of the flesh to the Fallen Angel waiting at the end of the derelict, litter-strewn alley.*

(For those who have not yet realised, Suck and Suck Again is yet another classic from the erotic showcase of Elissa Rand who sucked her way to the top of the hardcore pack in First Come First Served, Lift Girl, Suckers *and* Piranha Sex Tank.*)*

The WOMAN *moves like oiled silk to the head of a short flight of stone steps, a short trip down to nowhere. A blocked off exit to a pool hall.*

She turns, takes a last pull on the King Size Camel and grinds the butt into the dirt with her five-inch stiletto. She picks her way down the stone steps . . . The YOUTH *follows.*

Feature WAD SHOT *as the* YOUTH *walks down the steps.*

She grabs the YOUTH, *pins him against a highly durable heavy duty black plastic dustbin. She takes a dive. She's on her way down and we're about to discover what makes this woman's tonsils the Mecca Erotica of five continents.*

There's pulsing meat beyond the groaning zip. She pulls . . . CUT IN CLOSE on the Crimson Lips. Something deeply pornographic is about to take place, but a shadow blots out the screen.

Boos and jeers.

> CHRISTINE
> Turn on the light. Danielle, turn the light on.

The light from the Super-8 projector shines in CHRISTINE's face.

DANIELLE, *a transvestite dedicated to the transformation but failing abysmally, turns on the light. Grouped round the projector is a happy, homely group of MEN and what CHRISTINE calls her GIRLS. WC MORTEN, wearing a commissionaire's hat and coat, operates the projector.*

Most of the MEN are well into their fifties, some older, very much of the British Legion classes. Moderate men who vote Conservative and still think of Burtons as the fifty-shilling tailors. A good portion of them wear half-frame glasses and pullovers selected by their wives.

Several familiar faces among the men: MR POPOZOGOLOU, MR MARSDEN, MR DUNKLEY, MAC, MR WEBB, MR GRIVAS, *the estate agent, and SEVERAL OTHER MEN.*

Also, there's HARRY, *a jolly man in a wheelchair.*

Sitting with the MEN are three of the dozen 'GIRLS' at the party. JENNY *(26), rather plain, dressed as a schoolgirl,* HELEN *(25), black, wearing a tight dress.*

> CHRISTINE
> You shouldn't be watching this, not yet.

Objections from the CROWD.

> WC MORTEN
> They can't wait, Madam.

> JENNY
> We want to see the films.

General agreement. JENNY *is sitting with her arm round* MR FRANCIS, *a short, homely-looking man in his early seventies. The doorbell rings, quite persistent.*

> CHRISTINE
> (moving to the door)
> There's going to be a lesbian display first. The blue films are for later. There's *Hot Pussies, Horse Lovers, The Way to Valhalla.*

WC MORTEN
And *Casanova and the Nuns*.

CHRISTINE
— and the Nuns — but there's going to be a real live lesbian display first.

There are lots of PEOPLE in the house. A party is in progress.

MUSIC starts up from the gramophone — Pepe Jaramillo and His Latin American Rhythm.

There is a large through-lounge. A Capo di Monte world, ornate china statuettes on the mantelpiece, a reproduction of 'The Blue Boy' on the wall, a large sofa covered in wine coloured velvet, heavy drape curtains and a stuffed cat (not actual).

The party is not so much sensational as faintly incongruous. The MEN outnumber the WOMEN by approx. three to one. At one end of the lounge there is a small conservatory where drinks are being served from a makeshift bar by MAC and MR WEBB.

Snacks are being served by NICOLE, a man, dressed as a French maid. Being 6'1" in his socks, NICOLE towers above all of the guests in his high-heel shoes.

CHRISTINE is very happy, in her element. She walks from the lounge into the hallway. There is a queue of GENTLEMEN on the stairs waiting for a room to come free.

CHRISTINE
No sex in the bathroom, please. Last time, somebody pulled the sink off the wall.

MR GARDNER (76) is being helped down the stairs by DIANE (31), a very friendly person with wild hair and a big smile.

DIANE
Come on, that's it.

MR GARDNER
I'm all right.

The doorbell rings yet again.

CHRISTINE opens the front door to MR SHAH and MR PATEL, two Indian businessmen.

CHRISTINE
Hello! Come in.

MR SHAH
(perfect English)
My dear Christine, hello. This is my friend and colleague, Mr Patel.

CHRISTINE
Hello, come in. Is this the one who's getting me the fridge.

MR SHAH
This is the one.

MR PATEL
(also with perfect English)
We offer the best discounts in town, Miss Painter,
anything you want.

CHRISTINE
Except sex, eh?
(she laughs)
Brothel days is Mondays, Wednesdays and Fridays, but
this is just a party — a sex party. Enjoy yourself.

MR SHAH, *having taken out his wallet, hands over some notes to*
CHRISTINE.

MR SHAH
Who have we got here this evening?

CHRISTINE *takes the money.*

CHRISTINE
Helen's here. And Barbara.

MR SHAH
She's nice.

CHRISTINE
Oh, yes, and there's Fay . . .
(loud whisper)
No charge, she only does it in her spare time. She's really
a vet. That's her.

FAY *(38), short and dark, runs up the stairs and turns and smiles — a certain*
manic gleam in her eye.

CHRISTINE
She's fantastic. At my last party she held a special
gang-bang for the octogenarians. As many as you want,
whatever you want, wherever you want it. Here —

She gives them both a 15p luncheon voucher. Explains to MR PATEL.

CHRISTINE
When you go upstairs you hand this in to the girl. Don't
pay the girl, I pay them later. They hand in the vouchers.
Nicole! Get these gentlemen a drink. There's going to be a
real live lesbian show in a minute.

NICOLE *curtseys and offers* MR SHAH *and* MR PATEL *a drink. To*
applause, down the stairs comes the golden vision of EX-WING COM-

MANDER MORTEN *dressed, one would guess, as a Turkish belly dancer. His face is covered by a veil and his bald head by a wig.*

> CHRISTINE
> Silly bugger – what do you think you're doing?

WC MORTEN *follows* CHRISTINE *into the lounge.*

> WC MORTEN
> I am on a quest, Madam, searching for the perfect expression of my femininity. Not easy for an ageing pillock.

'I Shot the Sheriff' is playing on the gramophone. The WC launches into the dance of the seven veils.

> CHRISTINE
> Why can't you grow old gracefully, silly sod?

> WC MORTEN
> Certainly not, Madam, I intend to grow old disgracefully.

---

62   INT.   KITCHEN/CHRISTINE'S HOUSE   NIGHT

Later.

The party has quietened down. Somewhere in the background, James Last is playing 'Music for Lovers'.

CHRISTINE *is cooking poached eggs, helped by* MAC, *who is buttering the toast and pouring the tea.*

Seated round the formica kitchen table, eating poached eggs, hot toast and steaming hot mugs of tea, are MR GARDNER *(76),* HARRY, *in his wheelchair, the homely* MR FRANCIS *and* WC MORTEN – *now wearing a rather plain green dress and a lady's hat, such as those purchased by elderly ladies from stores like Dickins and Jones.*

HELEN, *looking tired, sits up on one of the worktops drinking tea and smoking a cig.*

CHRISTINE *serves a plate of eggs to* MR FRANCIS.

> CHRISTINE
> Here. Straight from the chicken's gonger.

> MR FRANCIS
> Thank you, Christine, you're a dear.

> WC MORTEN
> A beacon among the rocks.

> CHRISTINE
> Among the cocks, more like.

They chuckle.

> CHRISTINE
> (winks at Helen)
> Dirty old sods, every one of you.

> WC MORTEN
> What's the point of being old if you can't be dirty?

The OTHERS nod agreement.

Silence. The FOUR MEN eat their poached eggs. CHRISTINE sips her tea.

> HARRY
> (after a pause)
> Good party.

---

63   EXT.   CHRISTINE'S HOUSE   NIGHT
_____

The lid is lifted off the dustbin.

The contents – beercans, used tissues, used contraceptives, a bra, etc. – are transferred to a black plastic bag.

---

64   EXT.   THE BACK GARDEN   DAWN
_____

Dawn.

The birds are singing.

WC MORTEN stands in the back garden contemplating the dawn. A potentially poignant moment.

He is still wearing the rather plain green dress and the lady's hat. And he has removed his false teeth – top and bottom sets.

CHRISTINE walks out of the conservatory to see what the WC is up to.

> WC MORTEN
> It's a lovely morning, Madam.

> CHRISTINE
> You should be in bed.

> WC MORTEN
> Plenty of time for sleep, Madam, when I'm dead.

> CHRISTINE
> Look at the sight of you, silly sod. Get in before somebody calls an ambulance.

> WC MORTEN
> Silly old sod, indeed. At my age, Madam, fall asleep in public with one's teeth out, wake up in the loony bin.

CHRISTINE
And look at the state of the garden. Wot no slaves, what?
Where are they?

WC MORTEN
Waiting to worship and serve, O imperious lady.

CHRISTINE
Then take my knickers off and get your bum into gear. Get
busy.

She goes back into the house.

WC MORTEN
(proclaims)
'Let others hail the rising sun,
I bow to those whose course is run.'

He farts.

---

65   INT.   LOUNGE/CHRISTINE'S HOUSE   DAY

Afternoon.

CHRISTINE *lights the candles on a beautiful birthday cake in the shape of the number 16. It is* DAVID*'s birthday.*

Seated round a small table are DAVID, DOLLY, MAC, SHIRLEY *(dressed as the Governess); and the* EX-WING COMMANDER, *wearing a cardboard party pirate's hat, but otherwise dressed normally for a change – he even has his teeth in.*

SHIRLEY *puts her hands on* DAVID*'s shoulders, gives him a kiss.*

CHRISTINE
Right. Ready.

They all sing 'Happy Birthday'. Through the conservatory window three MALE SLAVES *can be seen slaving in the garden.* DAVID *blows out the candles.* EVERYBODY *applauds. 'Happy Birthday', etc.*

CHRISTINE
Right. Here.

CHRISTINE *takes* DAVID*'s hand and leads him out into the hall and up the stairs.*

She opens the bedroom door. The door swings slowly open to reveal CAROL *– a very beautiful woman with acres of red hair.*

CAROL
Hello, David.

CHRISTINE
This is Carol. Happy birthday.

She gives DAVID *a shove into the room and closes the door.*

CHRISTINE *stands outside the bedroom door, tears in her eyes. She takes out her hanky – click! – the bathroom door opens.*

> CHRISTINE
> Oh!

> MR MARPLES
> I'm sorry. Did I startle you?

Standing in the bathroom doorway is MR MARPLES, *in three-piece suit, carrying his large briefcase, but with his schoolboy cap on his head.*

> CHRISTINE
> I thought you'd gone.

> MR MARPLES
> I must be getting under way.

> CHRISTINE
> (notices the cap)
> Yes, you must.

CHRISTINE *follows* MR MARPLES *down the stairs.* SHIRLEY *is waiting in the hall.*

> MR MARPLES
> Thank you so much. Same time next week.

> SHIRLEY
> Yes. I'd take that off if I were you.

She removes the cap. MARPLES *stuffs it into his briefcase.* CHRISTINE *represses an attack of the giggles.*

> MR MARPLES
> Oh, thank you. Next week then.

SHIRLEY *opens the front door to find –*

> SHIRLEY
> (stern, to Mr Marples)
> Three o'clock, prompt.

– RALPH *(35), a commercial salesman. He is holding a garden rake and a pair of wellington boots.* RALPH *makes room for the massive* MR MARPLES *as he exits.* CHRISTINE *and* SHIRLEY *break up into giggles – leaving* RALPH *standing on the doorstep.*

> RALPH
> Hello.

> CHRISTINE
> (suddenly turns on Ralph)
> Hello?! You're late!

RALPH
I'm sorry, Mistress Christine, I've been to work.

CHRISTINE *grabs a riding crop from the hall stand.*

CHRISTINE
Work?! There's work to be done here, my boy. In!

She gives RALPH *a whack on the arse with the riding crop. He enjoys it.*

CHRISTINE
Come on, slave, get a move on.

CHRISTINE *whacks* RALPH *out into the garden, where he joins* PHIL *(28) and two other* SLAVES, *all wearing wellies and holding forks. The garden has undergone a considerable transformation.*

At this moment the SLAVES *are enjoying a glass of lemonade and a slice of birthday cake served from a tray by the* EX-WING COMMANDER.

CHRISTINE
What's this — the Queen's garden party? Get busy, you lot!

The SLAVES *hurry back to digging and weeding.* CHRISTINE *walks down the garden path, swishing the riding crop — she is more than aware of the devastating effect her high-heel shoes and stockings have on* PHIL *as he kneels weeding the border.*

WC MORTEN
Madam, they want to know, how much?

CHRISTINE
What for?

WC MORTEN
For digging the garden.

CHRISTINE
They're slaves . . . I thought it was free.

WC MORTEN
No, Madam, they want to know how much you want . . . for letting them dig the garden.

CHRISTINE
(thinks about it)
They've got to work much harder —
(turns to go)
or I won't accept a penny.

SLAVES
(as she goes)
Sorry, Mistress Christine.

CHRISTINE *walks back towards the house, through the conservatory, and into the lounge to find* SHIRLEY *and* DOLLY *– looking serious – the mood has changed.*

SHIRLEY
Christine.

CHRISTINE
What is it?

SHIRLEY *nods towards the hallway.* CHRISTINE *walks into the hallway to find . . .*

CHRISTINE
. . . Dad.

A considerable shock. EDWARD PAINTER *looks pale – hostile and defensive. Silence. He glowers at* CHRISTINE.

EDWARD
So this is it.

CHRISTINE
That's right. This is it. Take a good look.

EDWARD
I'm not here for a row.

CHRISTINE
That makes a change.

EDWARD
(shakes his head)
It doesn't matter which side I stand, I'm always on the wrong side of you. It's not easy.

CHRISTINE
Then why bother?

EDWARD
I need a woman.

CHRISTINE
(shocked)
Pardon?

EDWARD
(looking her in the eye)
A woman. Your father needs a woman.

CHRISTINE, *for once, is speechless. They stare at each other for some moments, the tension still there. Click! The door to the upstairs bedroom opens. Attention is suddenly directed to the top of the stairs. Footsteps.* DAVID *appears at the top of the stairs, all smiles.*

DAVID
Thank you, Mum.

CHRISTINE
Your grandfather's here, David.

DAVID *walks down the stairs.*

> **EDWARD**
> Hello, son.

> **DAVID**
> Hello.

> **CHRISTINE**
> Grandpa.

> **DAVID**
> Grandpa.

EDWARD *takes out his wallet, removes a £20 note, offers it to* DAVID.

> **EDWARD**
> Here. Happy birthday.

CHRISTINE *breaks into tears, embraces her* FATHER. *Tears in his eyes, he holds his* DAUGHTER. CHRISTINE *grabs* DAVID, *pulls him into the embrace. A reconciliation of three generations.*

> **CHRISTINE**
> Dad!

CAROL *appears at the top of the stairs, as beautiful as ever.* CHRISTINE *dries her eyes, blows her nose.*

> **CHRISTINE**
> Dad . . . Excuse us, David.
> (takes her father's hand)
> Come with me, Dad.

CHRISTINE *leads her* FATHER *up the stairs towards* CAROL. *Halfway up,* EDWARD *stops, turns to look at* DAVID, *realising what has happened.* DAVID *smiles.* EDWARD – *not at all sure that he approves.*

> **CHRISTINE**
> Up or down?

EDWARD *hesitates, looks at* CAROL, *then continues up the stairs.*

> **CHRISTINE**
> Dad – this is Carol. Carol – this is my Dad.

> **CAROL**
> (offers her hand)
> How do you do, Mr Painter?

> **EDWARD**
> (shakes her hand)
> How do you do?

> **CAROL**
> Very well.

CAROL *takes* EDWARD's *hand, leads him towards the bedroom.* CHRISTINE, *tears in her eyes, walks down the stairs to her son,* DAVID.

66   EXT.   CHRISTINE'S HOUSE   NIGHT

HIGH SHOT of the house. Everything is silent. Then:

MUSIC: Harry Belafonte sings 'Mary's Boy Child'. Followed by the:

TRANSFORMATION into CHRISTMAS. An illuminated tree in the window, fairy lights round the front porch, a Christmas wreath on the front door.

67   INT.   THE LOUNGE/CHRISTINE'S HOUSE   NIGHT

Harry Belafonte goes on singing as a makeshift curtain is pulled back to reveal a heavenly vision:

An ANGEL with golden hair, a golden halo and golden wings. A rare beauty. The ANGEL's wings are draped round her heavenly body, a cloak of liquid gold.

The wings begin to quiver, the ANGEL throws back her head and spreads wide her wings ecstatically revealing the full and glorious beauty of her body. An exotic, erotic vision. The ANGEL dances around the room.

Loud cheers and applause from the large CROWD OF PEOPLE gathered together for CHRISTINE's Christmas Party. The house has been beautifully decorated for this festive celebration.

> CHRISTINE
> (her voice cuts through the noise)
> Right, thank you, Larina! Now then, you lot. Come on,
> Webby, I want a snap of the girls.
> (shoves the men out of the way)
> You two, shift your gongers.

CHRISTINE *organises the 'GIRLS' into a group to pose for a photograph. There's at least twenty 'GIRLS' at the party, including most of the faces seen at the last party.*

EVERYBODY *wears party hats and carries streamers, ready to throw the moment the photograph is taken.* CHRISTINE *is having a wonderful time. This Christmas party is the high point of her year.*

> CHRISTINE
> Come on, you lot, stop pissing about and get into this
> picture! Carol — get your boobs in here. Jenny — look at the
> knickers.

MR WEBB *and* MR MARPLES *are at this party, though* MR MARPLES *stays discreetly in the background.* DANIELLE, *still looking distinctly masculine, wearing a short leatherette skirt and boots, gets into the picture. So does* NICOLE, *dressed as the French maid.* SHIRLEY *and* DOLLY *are there, they get pulled into the picture.* ROSE *is there, looking quite smart in a long black velvet dress. And* GLORIA, *large and formidable, a tattooed lady in a long leather dress.*

> CHRISTINE
> Gloria. Come on, Helen. Nicole, in at the back, please —
> very much so. Where's Dolly?

> DOLLY
> I'm here.

> CHRISTINE
> Danielle! Bloody cheer up. She's so dull.

> WC MORTEN
> Me too, Madam.

> CHRISTINE
> Not bloody likely.

The EX-WING COMMANDER *is dragged up as a French maid, including elbow length white gloves and twisted, laddered fishnet tights. He is wearing a blonde wig and a veil. He looks a wreck.*

> WC MORTEN
> Yes please, Madam.

> SHIRLEY
> Come on, Wing Commander.

THE EX-WING COMMANDER *gets into the picture.*

MR DUNKLEY
What about the men?

CHRISTINE
No men.

Objections, arguments, laughter. FAY and CAROL grab MR GARDNER (76) and sit him in front while somebody else wheels in HARRY in his wheelchair. LIONEL, in his gymslip, finds a place without CHRISTINE seeing him.

CHRISTINE
Right. That's it.

MR WEBB of the Inland Revenue takes the photograph. The screen is packed with an exotic collection of happy, smiling faces over which, standing on a chair at the back, the ANGEL spreads her golden wings.

CHRISTINE
One ... two ... three ...

EVERYBODY
(yells, waving their arms)
SEX!!!

Click! The photograph. Everybody laughs and cheers and kisses. CAROL gives HARRY a big French kiss. FAY lays on the same for MR GARDNER.

EVERYBODY
Happy Christmas! Happy Christmas!

CHRISTINE
Let the fucking commence!

EVERYBODY cheers. CAMERA moves in CLOSE on the happy, joyful face of CHRISTINE. Streamers fly as:

---

68   EXT.   THE HOUSE   NIGHT
_____

MUSIC: Herb Alpert's Tijuana Christmas.

HIGH SHOT: the house, front garden, gate and the road. A police car drives into shot, stops outside the house. Then another police van, then two more. Also a police car and two Ford Cortinas.

ASSORTED POLICEMEN and WOMEN pile out of the vehicles, some in plain clothes, some in uniform. They carry sledgehammers, torches and cameras. Some of them lean on the side door which leads into a passage through to the back garden. The door gives way easily.

HILLARD, JONES and TIMMS (all in plain clothes) and (in uniform) SUPERINTENDENT LENNOX (53) and SERGEANT GLOSSOP – a large man who comes from Yorkshire – all stride up to the front door. Behind

them, POLICEMEN *with sledgehammers.* LENNOX *bangs on the front door. On the other side,* CHRISTINE *begins to open the door. The door is on a safety chain.*

> **CHRISTINE**
> Who is it?

> **LENNOX**
> I am a police officer, I have a warrant to enter these premises. Open up.

CHRISTINE *slams the door shut.* SERGEANT GLOSSOP *puts his shoulder against the door and it gives way.*

A moment of panic, then CHRISTINE *goes into action, showing remarkable presence of mind throughout.*

> **CHRISTINE**
> Look out, everyone! It's a raid.

The POLICE *burst into the house. Suddenly, the* POLICE *are everywhere, piling in from every entrance.* DIANE, *naked, is half-way down the stairs.*

She turns and runs back up the stairs.

> CHRISTINE
> (to the police)
> Oh, well, you might as well come in now you're here.
> (to Timms)
> Nice to see you again.

> TIMMS
> This way.
> (heads up the stairs)
> Nobody move!

There's at least a dozen MEN queueing on the stairs, most of them are wearing party hats. HELEN screams. Total confusion as the MEN try to escape. FAY runs out of the lounge, dressed in only a red bra and panties.

> FAY
> Oh . . . men!

Herb Alpert plays on . . .

CUT TO:

THE BACK GARDEN: CLIENTS make a dash down the garden – The Great Escape revisited – but they are headed off by the POLICE. More POLICE come storming over the fence at the bottom of the garden. More than a raid – an invasion!

CUT TO:

OUTSIDE A BEDROOM:

> TIMMS
> We are police officers! Open up!

A POLICEMAN takes down the door with a sledgehammer. Six POLICEMEN and TIMMS burst into the room. MR GARDNER (76) is busy on the bed with CAROL (26).

> TIMMS
> We are police officers. Stop what you are doing.

> MR GARDNER
> I don't care who you are, I'm not stopping now.

CUT TO:

THE HALLWAY: More POLICEMEN and WOMEN pour in through the front door.

> CHRISTINE
> Come on in, boys. And you, girls, we're a bit short of girls.

CUT TO:

A BEDROOM: A POLICEMAN takes a picture of MR GARDNER and CAROL, now sitting up in bed together – smiling.

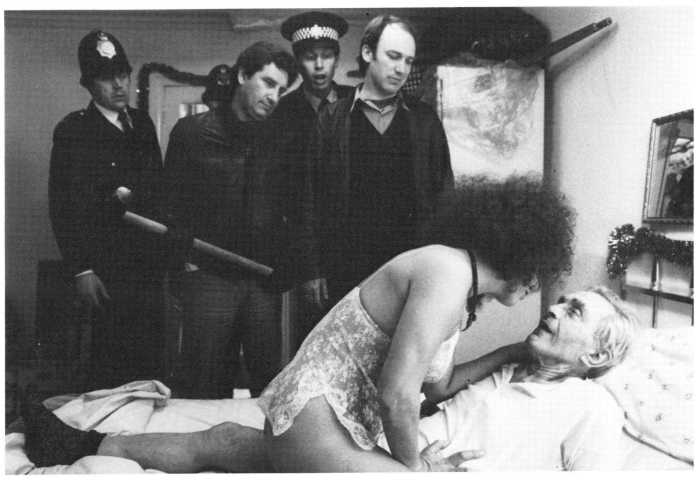

CUT TO:

ANOTHER BEDROOM: GLORIA *turns as* SUPERINTENDENT LENNOX *and three* POLICEMEN *burst into the room.* GLORIA *is holding a cat-o'-nine-tails.*

>   LENNOX
> Arrest this woman! That is an offensive weapon.

A noise from the wardrobe. LENNOX *pulls open the door to find* MR WEBB, *hiding, dressed in his favourite bikini.*

>   LENNOX
> Out!

CUT TO:

YET ANOTHER BEDROOM: Three POLICEWOMEN *and three* POLICEMEN *pull the covers off* DIANE *and* JENNIE *to reveal* MR MARSDEN *cowering beneath the sheets. A* POLICEMAN *takes a*

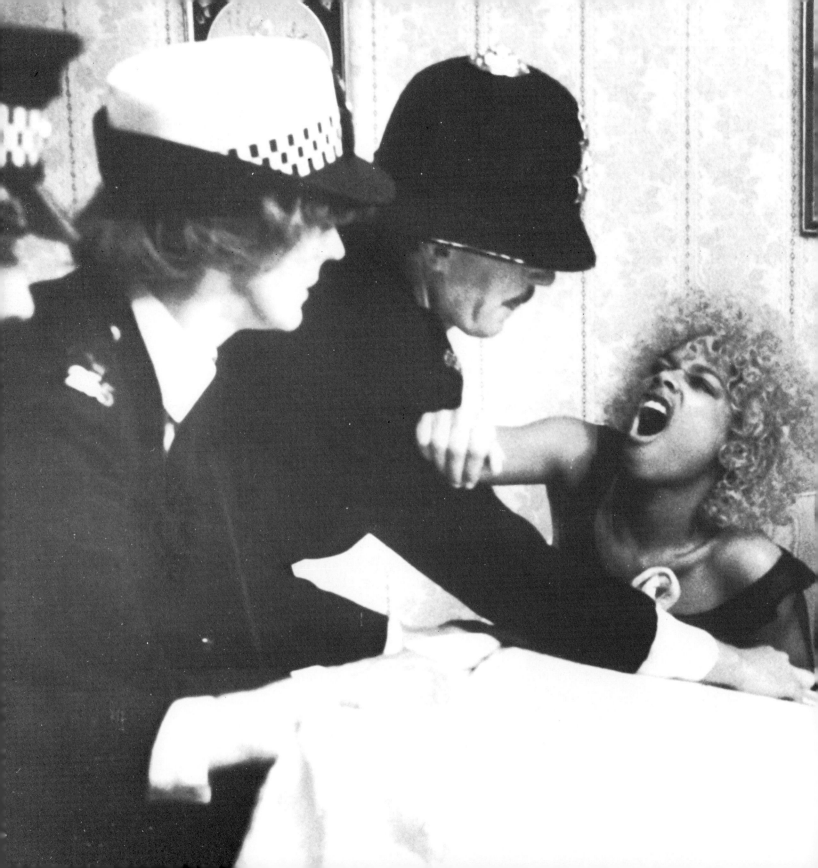

photograph. DIANE *and* JENNIE *smile and wave,* MR MARSDEN *covers his head.*

CUT TO:

IN THE LOUNGE: As LENNOX *and* GLOSSOP *come into the lounge, three* POLICEMEN *lead out* WC MORTEN. *He is singing 'Rule Britannia' in a high-pitched voice, but, under the surface, is very angry.*

> WC MORTEN
> (as he goes)
> Sod 'em all, Madam. I am a pervert — hip, hip, hip hooray.
>
> CHRISTINE
> (to Lennox)
> Do you have to knock down the doors?
>
> JONES
> This is the woman and these are the premises on which I have kept observation over the last three months. This house has been operating as a brothel during that time.
>
> LENNOX
> (to Christine)
> You have heard the officer. What have you to say?
>
> CHRISTINE
> If I'd have known he was out there all that time, I'd have asked him in for a cup of tea.

CUT TO:

IN A BEDROOM: evidence – Durex, tissues, vibrators, Crowe's Cremine – is swept from the bedside cabinet into a plastic bin bag.

CUT TO:

IN THE GARDEN: LENNOX *opens a coal bunker to find bondage equipment.*

CUT TO:

IN THE LAV: MARPLES, *dressed as the schoolboy, hides in the lav.*

CUT TO:

A BEDROOM: a pile of sex mags are put into a bin bag.

CUT TO:

IN THE HALLWAY: MEN *and* WOMEN *in various states of undress, are led out of the house by the* POLICE.

As MR SHAH *and* MR PATEL *are led out of the house:*

> LENNOX
> (stops them)
> Diplomats?

> MR SHAH
> I beg your pardon?

> LENNOX
> Are you diplomats?

> MR SHAH
> (catches on quickly, adopts an Indian accent)
> Oh, yes please, diplomats. Us. Yes. No scandals please.

> LENNOX
> (to Shah and Patel)
> Scarper!

> MR SHAH
> Yes, Sahib.

> MR PATEL
> Thank you.

MR SHAH *and* MR PATEL *are allowed to scarper.*

CUT TO:

OUTSIDE THE HOUSE: the road has been cordoned off. MEN *and* WOMEN *are being loaded into vans.* A CROWD *has gathered to watch. The 'GIRLS' wave, some of the* MEN *hide their faces. A cheer for* CHRISTINE *as she is led out by the* POLICE.

CHRISTINE *sees the black maria.*

> CHRISTINE
> I'm not going in that.

She sees a neighbour.

> CHRISTINE
> Hello, Maureen, we've been raided.
> (to Superintendent LENNOX)
> I hope you're going to apologise to the neighbours for this.

> LENNOX
> (tired)
> Don't make trouble.

> CHRISTINE
> I'm not going in no black maria like some common
> criminal.

> LENNOX
> Everyone else is.

> CHRISTINE
> I'll go in yours. Which one's yours?

> LENNOX
> (sighs)
> Oh, very well.

LENNOX *opens the back door of the police car for* CHRISTINE, *and* CHRISTINE *gets in.*

> CHRISTINE
> He's a gentleman. Just my type. Got a touch of royalty about him.

CUT TO:

IN THE LAV: the door is bashed down. MARPLES *cowers.* TIMMS, HILLARD *and two* POLICEMEN *dive on* MARPLES, *engulfing him in a large plastic dustbin bag.*

Herb Alpert's Tijuana Christmas scratches to a halt.

CUT TO:

IN THE GARDEN: HIGH SHOT. The ANGEL *runs into the garden, flapping her golden wings. She is chased by two* POLICEMEN *who bring her down with a rugger tackle.*

CUT TO:

OUTSIDE THE HOUSE: POLICEMEN *struggle as they try to get* HARRY *in his wheelchair into one of the vans.*

---

69   INT.   THE POLICE STATION   NIGHT

All the MEN *have been brought to the police canteen.*

Having been literally caught with their collective trousers down, the MEN *would do anything to get out of here.* DANIELLE, NICOLE *and* WC MORTEN *look incongruous in their female clothing.* JONES *stands on a chair.*

> JONES
> Gentlemen, I would ask you to be patient.

> WC MORTEN
> (like a sheep)
> Baa!

Resplendent in his tatty French maid's uniform, EX-WING COMMAN-DER MORTEN *also climbs on to a chair and begins to bleat like a sheep.*

> JONES
> Tea and baked beans will be served and statements will be taken. We won't keep you long.

He nods to three POLICEMEN *who make a dive for* WC MORTEN.

WC MORTEN
(as he is led off)
Baa! Baa! You're all a lot of sheep! You don't need to give statements. What's the charge?! Ask them what's the charge! You're all a lot of sheep! Baa!

70   INT.   CORRIDOR/POLICE STATION   NIGHT

SERGEANT GLOSSOP *walks along the corridor passing interview rooms into which* WOMEN *are being placed, isolated one from another.* DOLLY, *remaining cool, is escorted into one of the rooms.*

GLOSSOP *is carrying two mugs of tea. He goes into an interview room where* CHRISTINE *is waiting.*

SERGEANT GLOSSOP
What a carry-on, eh?

71   EXT.   TOOTING BEC COMMON   NIGHT

A remote corner of Tooting Bec Common. A police van stops. HILLARD *and* TIMMS *open the back of the van and pull out* MR MARPLES. *Plastic bin bag on his head, he is thrust on to the common. The van drives off.*

Still in his schoolboy outfit, MARPLES *struggles to get out of the bin bag. He spins to see where he is. Hanging on a tree in front of him, he sees his suit, shirt, shoes, etc.*

72   INT.   THE POLICE CELLS   NIGHT

JONES *and three* POLICEMEN *escort the* EX-WING COMMANDER *to the cells.*

WC MORTEN
I am a retired officer of the RAF. Twice decorated. I flew two hundred and seven missions over occupied territory. In bra and panties.

JONES
You're a disgrace.

WC MORTEN
This is no way to treat a lady.

The cell door slams behind the EX-WING COMMANDER.

SERGEANT GLOSSOP *and* CHRISTINE *sit at a table drinking their mugs of tea.*

CHRISTINE
It's just like a Tupperware party, really, but I sell sex instead of plastic containers. If the wives were willing, I'd be out of a job, wouldn't I? They go off sex — rather sell Tupperware. Ha, bloody ha.
(she laughs)
Sex soon goes out of a marriage. I'm a bit old-fashioned really. I believe in marriage. Men are animals, sexually. They don't talk a bit of sense until you've got them despunked. Women are more affectionate, they like a bit of affection — though I've met a few horny buggers in my time. The wife wants a three-piece suite. If she gave the man sex he might be more inclined to come across with the three-piece suite. It may not be a fashionable thing to say but, once you've got him despunked and he's sitting there thinking he's all wonderful, done you a good turn, giving you a pair of soggy knickers, in the afterglow of his glory he's more likely to come across with the Dralon three-piece, don't you think?

SERGEANT GLOSSOP
You may well be right, love, I don't know. Personally I've been married twenty years and we still go at it like rabbits.

SUPERINTENDENT LENNOX *comes into the interview room, followed by* TIMMS.

CHRISTINE
(to Lennox)
I'm responsible. Not the men. You can't expect the men to be responsible. When the balls are full the brain is empty. Ask him.
(meaning Timms)
I'm fully responsible.

LENNOX
We'll be looking to make several charges, including possessing obscene articles for gain, selling liquor without a licence, running a disorderly house and keeping a brothel.

CHRISTINE
I just perform a service.

TIMMS
You'll go down for this.

CHRISTINE
I only go down for a price, dear, and I doubt if you could afford it.

74   EXT.   POLICE STATION   NIGHT

HIGH SHOT. One by one, all the MEN *leave the police station and go their separate ways.*

They disappear into the night. Two POLICEMEN *carry* HARRY *out of the station in his wheelchair. He pushes his way off into the shadows. Hold on this shot before moving into* . . .

75   EXT.   CHRISTINE'S HOUSE   DAY

LAWSON, *a reporter, leans on the doorbell. No response. He kneels and looks through the letter-box. Sees nothing.*

LAWSON *stands back and looks up at the windows on the upper floor. Having hung around for several hours, he and the several other* RE-PORTERS *outside the front gate are more or less of the opinion that there is nobody in the house.*

He presses his nose against the window, net curtains shroud any clear view of the inside of the house. Then – Boo! A shock for LAWSON. *Suddenly there is a face, as close to the glass on the inside of the window as is his face on the outside.*

WC MORTEN, *neatly and normally dressed, except for a toy policeman's helmet, wags his finger at* LAWSON. WC MORTEN *points his finger towards the front door. The other* REPORTERS *move in on the action.*

WC MORTEN *still in the helmet opens the front door.*

> WC MORTEN
> Good morning, gentlemen! Please . . . please . . . no need to storm the fort!
>
> LAWSON
> Is Miss Painter here? Is she here?
>
> WC MORTEN
> No, Madam is not here but, if you would care to follow me, we will proceed with a conducted tour of the premises.

The REPORTERS, *having anticipated resistance, find this a quite unexpected invitation. They file into the house.*

WC MORTEN *leads the* REPORTERS *through the hall into the lounge.*

WC MORTEN
This way, please, this way.

REPORTER
Is it true she gave sex to people in wheelchairs?

WC MORTEN
There *was* a minimal charge, sir, but, yes, it is true.
Everything is true, sir. All in good time. My name is
Morten, ex-Wing Commander. Since my retirement, I have
devoted my life to transvestism and the pursuit of sexual
deviation and I am now a very happy man – having
escaped from an extremely overcrowded closet.
(he begins the tour)
Here – catering strictly for the tastes of the older
gentleman – here is the lounge where clients relaxed with
a bridge roll and a gin and tonic before going upstairs
with the lady of their choice – thus undermining the
moral fabric of the nation. But, let me take you to where I
know you are longing to go. Upstairs. To reveal the exotic
underbelly of our beloved country. Follow in the footsteps
of fathers and grandfathers, fornicators all.

He leads them out into the hall and up the stairs, stops and turns.

WC MORTEN
In each of the four bedrooms, including the deeply exotic
mirror room, on every bedside cabinet – tissues,
contraceptives, excitors, pulsators, pleasers and teasers,
liberal quantities of cold cream and other accoutrements
of the profession. If, in your innocence, there is anything
you do not understand, if there is anything you wish to
see, please do not hesitate to ask – for, in this house, we
have nothing to hide.

And, on into:

76   INT.   COURTROOM   DAY
___

CHRISTINE's *trial in the Crown Court. Everybody,* LAWYERS,
BARRISTERS, COURT OFFICIALS, *etc. is assembled in the court and
waiting for the arrival of the* JUDGE. WC MORTEN *and* SHIRLEY *sit
either side of* DOLLY *in the public gallery.*

CHRISTINE *is in the dock, her hair specially perm-waved for her trial, and
wearing a sober, well-tailored two-piece suit and blouse.*

CLERK OF THE COURT
Be upstanding in court!

EVERYBODY *stands.*

Enter the JUDGE.

The JUDGE, *fully attired in his official robes, enters the court. He takes his time getting to his seat, adjusting his papers, making himself comfortable.*

The JUDGE *looks up and we see, for the first time, the face of* JUSTICE MARPLES.

CUT TO:

CHRISTINE, *who reacts to this familiar face.*

CUT BACK, in close, on JUSTICE MARPLES, *but now dressed as the schoolboy, cap on head. Not a flicker of recognition.*

Back to CHRISTINE. *She smiles.*

Back in close on MARPLES, *once again in his Judge's attire. He stares directly at* CHRISTINE *as the* CAMERA *pulls slowly back to reveal, sitting to the left and right of* JUSTICE MARPLES, *two other* JUDGES, JUSTICE EDWARD PAINTER *and his son-in-law,* JUSTICE EDGAR WINTER.

SHOT WIDENS even further to reveal more and more JUDGES. *A crowd of* JUDGES. SYDNEY, TIMMS, MR POPOZOGOLOU, MR WEBB, MR MARSDEN, *all the other* CLIENTS, *the* POLICE, EVERYBODY – *all the* MEN *we have seen, all sitting in judgement on this one* WOMAN.

. . . All, that is, except EX-WING COMMANDER MORTEN, *World War II bomber ace. A Hero. Two hundred and seven missions over occupied territory . . . in bra and panties . . .*